David Roberts

FROM AN
ANTIQUE LAND

TRAVELS IN EGYPT AND THE HOLY LAND

Edited by Barbara Culliford
Foreword by Helen Guiterman

David Roberts
FROM AN
ANTIQUE LAND

TRAVELS IN EGYPT AND THE HOLY LAND

Weidenfeld and Nicolson
New York

In memory of Dora Charman 1915–1986

The editor and publishers wish to thank Dr Iain G. Brown, Assistant Keeper in the Department of Manuscripts of the National Library of Scotland, and Eddie Niessen, for their help in preparing this book.

Published by Weidenfeld & Nicolson, New York
A Division of Wheatland Corporation
841 Broadway
New York, New York 10003-4793

Published in Canada by General Publishing Company, Ltd.

Library of Congress Cataloging-in-Publication Data

Roberts, David, 1796–1864.
From an antique land.

1. Roberts, David, 1796–1864 — Diaries. 2. Lithographers — England — Diaries. 3. Egypt in art.
4. Palestine in art. I. Culliford, Barbara. II. Title.

NE2347.6.R62A2   1989   769.92'4   [B]   88-33770
ISBN 1-55584-350-6

From an Antique Land was conceived by Thames Head, a division of BLA Publishing Limited, East Grinstead, Sussex, England, a member of the Ling Kee Group.

Design: Maryann Rogers
Editorial: Sheila Mortimer

Phototypeset in Britain by BLA Publishing Limited/Composing Operations
Origination in The Netherlands, printed in Portugal

First American Edition
10 9 8 7 6 5 4 3 2 1

Contents

Foreword
by Helen Guiterman

I am pleased to write the Foreword to this book which reproduces some of the lithographs from the volumes which generally are known as *Egypt, Syria and the Holy Land*[1]. It is these lithographs, drawn on the stone by Roberts's friend Louis Haghe, whom he had known since the publication of *Picturesque Sketches of Spain* in 1837, that are the best known examples of Roberts's work. The standard of Haghe's lithography was very high, and the publication greatly enhanced his and Roberts's reputations, although it did not greatly enrich Roberts's pocket, as he was paid only £3,000 by his publisher. The lithographs were issued in monthly parts, later bound into volumes by their owners. It is impossible to know how many copies were printed; the list of subscribers totalled just over 600; they included Queen Victoria and other European royalties, Mehemet Ali, Pasha of Egypt, the Duke of Wellington and a number of other Lords and Ladies; others were John Ruskin, Charles Dickens, B.R. Haydon, J.G. Kinnear, John Murray, Thomas Seddon, Thomas Waghorn and Sir David Wilkie.

I assume that there were more copies printed than this. Roberts's celebrity did not rest only on these lithographs; from the moment of his return from the East — apart from going to Edinburgh to see his parents — he began to make use of his sketchbooks,

his watercolours, his oil studies and his drawings, to paint many canvasses of Eastern subjects. These caused a good deal of excitement, for they were not only effective as paintings, but portrayed scenes unknown to the vast majority of critics and writers, and of visitors to exhibitions. His first five Eastern oils were hung at the Royal Academy in 1840; next year, three were at the Academy and two at the British Institution; in 1861 he had a Baalbek subject at the Academy, the last of his Eastern exhibits, 21 years after his return. But he did not confine himself to eastern scenes during these years; he painted views of cities, of Roman ruins, and of churches and cathedrals in many lands. The *Art Journal*[2] wrote: 'It is not our belief that Roberts is appreciated or understood as a painter of sacred interiors .... We may seek through the past and through the present to find an artist who can call up the same feelings as Roberts moves within us on contemplating his church interiors ...'

Roberts was not a landscape painter, though inevitably landscape was a part of his architectural exteriors. He was in no sense a portraitist. He was a topographical and architectural artist, entirely self-taught; by looking at the works of his forebears and his contemporaries, he learnt. He was not necessarily accurate in his depictions, altering when he thought it would improve

them. His subjects and his style did not much change during his lifetime. F.T.Palgrave wrote: '... On the whole, hardly any difference is perceptible during his long and industrious career; the colouring is always dexterous, always generalised after a system of the artist's own, which one might describe as a kind of shorthand of natural effect ...'[3]

His facility grew with practice; early oils are sometimes heavy and clumsy. He has been accused of making his figures too small in order to make the buildings look larger; this is a well-known trick, used by architects and painters, including those of early Dutch interiors.

Roberts was an affable friendly man, popular among his contemporaries. He never lost his Scottish accent, nor did he forget old friends and was a kind benefactor to many poor artists. He had been born into a very poor family and first showed signs of talent by chalking on his mother's kitchen walls. This early ability led to his being apprenticed to a painter and decorator in Edinburgh, instead of following his father's trade as a shoemaker. After serving his seven years, he was employed as a house-painter of no mean skill, renowned for his marbling and wood imitations; more or less by chance he got a job as a scene-painter in Scotland. For a while he worked at both, house-painting when he had no theatrical work. Soon,

however, he was fully employed in the theatres of Glasgow and Edinburgh.

Roberts went to London in 1822, finding work first at the Royal Coburg, now the Old Vic, and soon at Drury Lane and Covent Garden Theatres. He worked often with Clarkson Stanfield: in an article in the *Art Journal* the writer commented: 'All who remember the beautiful series of *pictures*, for they could scarcely be called *scenes*, which the two artists produced at Drury Lane and Covent Garden Theatres, till 1830, must have felt how greatly these pictorial works influenced public taste in what was beautiful in scenic art, compared with what had previously existed ...'[4]. It is important to realise that scene-painters were then both designers and executants; many artists began their careers in just such a way. Roberts's theatre work often included elaborate effects such as moving dioramas and panoramas, sometimes for employers outside the theatre. He also carried out a redecoration scheme for the interior of Covent Garden Theatre, designing a Drop Curtain at the same time.

The Athenaeum commented: '... in the course of his work at the theatre he had acquired so extraordinary a power of painting and of covering large spaces of canvas in a short time, that he could be relied on to produce wonders even at the latest moment ... . Roberts was one of the most methodical of men, from the practice of his art to the arrangement of his studio, everything was in order ...'[5]. It has been often said that it was Roberts's training as a scene-painter that led to his rapidity of execution in easel painting. Might it not have been his ability to work quickly which made him a successful scenic artist?

At the same time as he was working hard in the theatre, he was painting watercolours and oils, exhibiting regularly, and providing many drawings to be engraved in the popular illustrated books of the day. He exhibited *Rouen Cathedral* at the Royal Academy in 1825, followed by other French and Belgian subjects; almost all were bought at once, and were noticed favourably by the critics; he had struck out a line of his own.

Over ten years before he went East, he

painted an imaginary scene in the same dramatic style as John Martin, called *The Israelites leaving Egypt*[6] (Society of British Artists, 1829). Another of these imaginary Eastern subjects was *The Destruction of Jerusalem by Titus*[7] (Royal Academy, 1847).

Roberts's travels had taken him to France, to the Low Countries and to Germany and, in October 1832, he went on his first long adventurous journey. He went to Spain where he spent eleven months, visiting the north, and travelling via Madrid to Cordova and Granada. From Gibraltar he crossed to Morocco, his first taste of Africa, and then he spent five months in Seville, finally driven away by an outbreak of cholera. Everywhere he went, he drew and occasionally he painted in oil. On his return, he wasted no time in securing contracts for illustrations for four issues of *The Landscape Annual*[8]; later he provided drawings for a book of 27 lithographs, *Picturesque Sketches of Spain*[9].

This Spanish journey served as a rehearsal for his later, more important, Eastern expedition. Not only did he experience hardship, but also he learned how to make the best use of his travels. Roberts spent the next few years painting Spanish subjects, which he had little difficulty in selling; the money he earned from these activities financed his Eastern expedition, dealt with by Barbara Culliford. I am glad that she has used

Roberts's lively original Journal, for many writers and lecturers use only the abbreviated and altered version in the 1866 biography, written by his friend James Ballantine[10].

On his return, Roberts found himself fully occupied; the watercolours of his Eastern tour were exhibited twice in London, and also in Edinburgh and Glasgow. The main aim was to obtain subscriptions for the

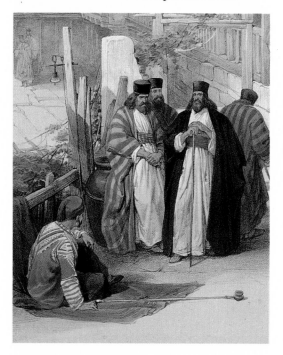

forthcoming books of lithographs, to be issued in monthly parts and in two sections, the first being *The Holy Land*, the second *Egypt*. He redrew each watercolour so that his lithographer could work from drawings which Roberts had perfected. The exhibitions of the original drawings received rapturous reviews, for example: 'The masterly skill and dexterity of hand with which Mr Roberts has delineated the characteristic features of the scenery and the minutest details of the architecture — combining breadth of effect and grandeur of size, with precision and neatness of outline and local colour — are the theme of universal admiration; it is surprising to observe the largeness of view which takes in with a comprehensive eye the broad masses of such stupendous subjects, united with the most careful exactness in delineating every hieroglyphic on the walls, and the coloured pattern of each individual capital. The artist has felt the sentiment of the scenes with the mind of a poet, and depicted them with the accuracy of a draughtsman; and we think it will be acknowledged that the stupendous proportions of Egyptian remains have never been adequately represented till now.'[11]

The Scotsman, reviewing the Edinburgh exhibition, commented: 'We do not think that modern enterprise has ... presented public curiosity and taste with any work ...

at all excelling the present. Indeed, for extent, design, execution, and above all for variety of interest, we can remember none with which to compare it ...[12]. The *Scottish Standard*: '... In the whole 150 drawings which we went over, not a blemish or slip of the pencil was discernible. His touch seems magical; for nothing is more remarkable in these drawings, each taken and coloured on the spot, than the infallibility of the artist's pencil ...'

Roberts was elected a full member of the Royal Academy on his return to England, when the *Morning Post* commented: '... Mr Roberts brought as much honour to the Academy (and perhaps more) as ever he could have received from that body. These his sketches will live forever ...'

The first part of *Egypt, Syria and the Holy Land* came out in 1842, and the *Egypt* section commenced publication in 1847. After his Eastern journey, and with the success of the lithographs, perhaps it might appear that the rest of Roberts's life was an anti-climax, but I don't think he found it so. He made a number of European tours, returning to Belgium and Holland and France several times. He went to North Italy for the first time in 1851, spending five weeks in Venice. In 1853–4 he wintered in Rome, returning by way of Naples. Apart from this, he went almost every year to

Scotland to see old friends and revisit his favourite places, usually to draw. He went often to the Isle of Wight, where his daughter and her husband had a house; he enjoyed being with his numerous grandchildren. His last visit to Belgium was in 1861 and his last to Paris in 1863.

Roberts enjoyed his celebrity; he exhibited regularly at the Royal Academy. Only in his last few years did he receive any adverse notices from the critics, but his paintings continued to sell.

Travelling so widely and producing many paintings and drawings would seem to be enough for one man, but not for Roberts; he prepared architectural drawings for a proposed new National Gallery, designed stained-glass windows for the Scott Monument in Edinburgh, for which, many years earlier, he had sent drawings which were rejected. He was always ready to do battle against proposed 'improvements' for Edinburgh or for his beloved Roslin Chapel. He arranged a memorial exhibition of the works of his friend William Etty at the Royal Society of Arts, and designed a scene for Charles Dickens's production of *Not so Bad as we Seem* in 1851. He was drawn into the controversy over the cleaning and hanging of Turner's paintings after his death, and gave evidence to the *Select Committee on the National Gallery* on the management and

restoration of the works in its collections. In short, he was not an idle man, finding time to meet friends at his Club, the Garrick, or at his home where he gave dinner parties for famous men such as Charles Dickens and William Thackeray, Sir Edwin Landseer and J.M.W. Turner. Many of his patrons became his friends and he stayed with them in their palatial houses; some of these were rich industrialists, some titled men. Queen Victoria and Prince Albert commissioned several works, and he went a number of times to see them at Windsor and at Osborne to dicuss the paintings.

Roberts, like many Victorian painters, famous in their day, suffered an eclipse at the time when all things Victorian were anathema. Like many others, he is now once again famous and commanding high prices.

F.T. Palgrave wrote: '... Looking at it as art, we may regard as the great merit of Roberts' style, its intelligibility; he leaves one in no doubt of what he thinks worth attention, making his object perfectly clear, and at the same time putting in just enough effect to raise it to the level of a picture ... . But Egyptian Roman Gothic are all alike in his work ... there is one sunlight upon them all — almost one atmosphere for Egypt or for England ...'[13].

Not everyone would agree with this comment, as, for instance, the writer of

The Times obituary who observed he was: '... a kindly, canny Scot, well-to-do, amazingly clever in his own sphere of art, and liked by all who knew him ... . He published more than one fine series of sketches ... which gave him a great public reputation ... . He was certainly the best architectural painter that our country has yet produced. In this department of art, indeed, he stands almost alone among us, the artist who comes next to him being Samuel Prout ... . Mr Roberts had a wonderfully quick eye for all striking effects of architecture, and transferred them to his canvas with great ease. Nothing can be more effective than his views of cathedral interiors lit up with the magnificent pageants of Roman Catholic religion. He gave a grand broad effect, a truthful general result, and did not much trouble himself with minuteness of workmanship ... . In this broad style of treatment Mr David Roberts was particularly happy, and he could be very prolific. He painted quickly and he painted much. His pictures were snapped up at heavy prices. If he fell short of genius he was, nevertheless, a man of rare ability, of sturdy industry, and of admirable tact. Like many Scotchmen he spoke slow with a broad accent, and gave one in conversation the idea of a slow-working intellect. In his art, however, there was nothing slow or drawling. Whatever he did he did quickly, sharply, and with marked vigour ... . He who began as a humble house-painter, and ended as a Royal Academician, has not a little to boast of. He too belongs to that proud phalanx of men whose biographies touch most keenly all young ambition — the self-made men who from small beginnings have fought their way upwards to fame, to wealth, and to station ...'[14].

Notes to Foreword

1. *The Holy Land, Syria, Idumea, Arabia, Egypt and Nubia*. F.G. Moon, London, 1842–49. A reduced size edition was published by Day & Son, London, 1855.
2. *Art Journal*, 1869, page 312.
3. F.T. Palgrave, *Gems of English Art of this Century*, George Routledge & Sons, London and New York, 1869, pages 78–82.
4. *Art Journal*, 1858, page 201. British Artists; Their Style and Character.
5. *The Athenaeum,* 2 December, 1864, page 746.
6. Birmingham City Museum and Art Gallery.
7. Whereabouts unknown.
8. *The Landscape Annual*, Robert Jennings & Co. London. Roberts illustrated four volumes, 1835–38.
9. *Picturesque Sketches of Spain*, Hodgson and Graves, London, 1837.
10. James Ballantine, *The Life of David Roberts R.A.* Edinburgh, 1866.
11. *The Spectator* (date unkown).
12. *The Scotsman,* 2 January, 1841.
13. F.T. Palgrave, *op. cit.*
14. *The Times,* 28 November, 1864, page 7.

Introduction

According to his friend and biographer James Ballantine, David Roberts regarded a trip to the Near East as 'the dream of his life from boyhood' and 'the central episode of his artistic life'. Roberts was attracted to the area after he had experienced Moorish architecture on his successful sketching trip to Spain and Morocco in 1832. As a professional artist, he was well aware of the potential commercial value of a portfolio of sketches of Egypt and the Holy Land. A working journey to the area became feasible with the development of steam travel and the greater political stability of the area under Mehemet Ali, Pasha of Egypt.

In August 1838, Roberts left London. He travelled through France to Marseilles where he joined a steamer bound for Malta. Here he changed steamers and headed for the Aegean where he boarded a ship sailing to Alexandria. The vessel was crowded with Turkish pilgrims on their way to Mecca and the lively atmosphere on board must have given Roberts an intriguing foretaste of what was to come in the Muslim countries on his itinerary. In Alexandria he hired a servant, ordered provisions for the expedition and began his sketching. Two days later he reached Cairo for a brief stop to arrange his transport up the Nile — a houseboat which cost £15 per month and had first to be sunk in order to rid it of rats. Most of Roberts's

sketches of Cairo were done when he returned to the city at the end of December.

The voyage up the Nile into Nubia was to prove uneventful and luxurious when compared with the journey by camel train across the wastes of Sinai. After visiting Saint Catherine's Monastery and the ruins of Petra, he reached Jerusalem and made the final part of his journey by horseback through the Holy Land to Baalbek. From Beirut, he sailed back to Alexandria where he finally met the Pasha of Egypt, Mehemet Ali, under whose protection he had been travelling.

The forty years of Roberts's own lifetime had seen tremendous developments in European awareness of the Near East, and of Egypt in particular. At the time of his birth in 1796, Egypt was a mysterious land, an impoverished province of the Ottoman Empire administered by Turkish pashas. Disease was rife and the area was hostile to the rare foreigners who ventured to visit it. Napoleon's expedition to Egypt in 1798 brought about a profound change. The purpose of his invasion was to cut England's route to India but he was defeated by the British and Turkish forces, and the French forces were marooned in Egypt until 1801. Accompanying the French military expedition were 167 scientists and scholars led by Baron Dominique Vivant Denon, and his account of his journey up the Nile in pursuit of Mameluke troops was published in 1802 with the title *Voyage dans la Basse et la Haute Egypte*. The scholars and scientists discovered the incredible heritage of Egypt and published their findings in *Description de l'Egypte*, a fully illustrated encyclopedia which began to appear in 1809. Napoleon's expedition discovered the Rosetta Stone in 1799 and although it was surrendered to the

British after the French defeat, impressions of the hieroglyphic inscriptions were first taken. The French scholar Champollion found the key to deciphering the hieroglyphics and this discovery, along with the Egyptian objects which were being brought back to European collections, led to the foundation of the science of Egyptology.

In 1821, an Egyptian exhibition was staged in London by Giovanni Battista Belzoni who was an Italian pioneer Egyptologist. This former circus strongman had travelled to Egypt in 1814, looking for employment with Mehemet Ali. The Pasha did not employ him but the British consul, Henry Salt, and the Swiss explorer, Jean Louis Burckhardt, commissioned him to lift the head of a statue of a pharaoh in Luxor and transport it down the Nile. This was the era of the adventurer archaeologists who removed what they could and shipped statues and obelisks to Europe. Belzoni worked for Salt for several years, excavating at the pyramids at Giza, the Valley of the Kings and Abu Simbel. A more scholarly approach followed, and John Gardiner Wilkinson, who arrived in 1821 from Britain, spent twelve years in the Nile Valley surveying the monuments and deciphering inscriptions. Several such surveys, using draughtsmen and architects, were carried out before Roberts arrived in Egypt but he

was the first artist to set out with the intention of recording the monuments for later commercial publication.

When Roberts arrived in Egypt in 1838, the major cities on his itinerary had resident British consuls. A friend had provided him with a Foreign Office letter of introduction to the consul in Alexandria, Colonel Campbell, who supplied Roberts with the necessary permits, a letter of introduction to the Pasha and access to funds. It was unusual at this time to travel alone and on the voyage up the Nile, Roberts joined forces with a wealthy

gentleman traveller, Mr Vanderhorst (nicknamed Pickwick), who was described thus in his Journal: Mr V is a gentleman who thinks travelling better for his health than staying at home. He takes with him a Maltese servant and an Italian cook who are indefatigable in their endeavours to serve him. Also accompanying Roberts were Captain Nelley who could speak Arabic, and an unidentified Mr A. These three did not travel with Roberts on the camel and horseback journey into the Holy Land but when he returned to Cairo from the Nile trip, he met

Pell and Kinnear who were planning a trip to Syria via Petra and Jerusalem. Pell was an experienced Middle Eastern traveller and Kinnear, a Scottish businessman, was to produce his own account of their travels, *Cairo, Petra and Damascus in 1839.*

Ibrahim Pasha, Mehemet Ali's adopted son, invaded Syria in 1831 and eventually control of a large part of Syria was seceded to Mehemet Ali. Travel in the Holy Land had thus become less hazardous although plague was still a problem.

Petra was rediscovered in 1812 by Jean Louis Burckhardt, the first European for centuries to visit the Nabatean ruins and report on his findings. To reach Petra had involved the Swiss explorer in great intrigue and personal danger but his discovery slowly led to more travellers making the journey, although it was still not on the pilgrim trail. An American theologian, Edward Robinson, visited the Holy Land shortly before Roberts and spent a day at Petra. His expedition to identify the sites of biblical events lasted for four months and in 1841 he published *Biblical Researches in Palestine, Mount Sinai and Arabia Petraea.* A series of picturesque etchings were drawn by the French engraver Linant after he had visited Petra in 1826. Roberts saw these engravings when he met the Frenchman in Egypt and was inspired to see the ruins for himself.

The interest aroused by recent archaeological discoveries and the increasing desire to visualise the geography of the Bible lands provided Roberts with an eager public for his material. He returned to London after an absence of 11 months with 272 sketches, a panorama of Cairo and three full sketchbooks. Roberts himself realised the importance of his work and felt that he had enough material on which to base a lifetime's work.

The pencil-written Journal was transcribed, at Roberts's request, into two leatherbound notebooks by his eighteen-year-old daughter Christine and this is now in the National Library of Scotland.

Publisher's note: the spelling in the Journal transcribed by Roberts's daughter is occasionally inconsistent and the modern reader may also find the sentence construction unusual. To preserve the flavour of the text, we have on the whole not altered the punctuation but spelling has been standardized where it might otherwise distract the reader.

David Roberts 1796–1864

1796	Born in Edinburgh
1815–22	After apprenticeship, employed in Scotland as house-painter, later as scene-painter
1822	To London
1822–30	Worked as scene-painter and began easel painting in earnest
1824	First works exhibited in London
1824–30	To France, Belgium, Holland and Germany
1832–33	Eleven months in Spain
1838	Elected Associate Member of the Royal Academy
1838–39	Eleven months in the East
1841	Elected Member of the Royal Academy
1842–49	*Egypt, Syria and the Holy Land* published in monthly parts
1843	To France, Belgium and Holland
1851	To Northern Italy for two months
1853–54	To Rome and Naples for six months
1860–64	Worked on a series of paintings *London from the Thames*
1861	To Belgium for a month
1863	To Paris for a month
1864	Death of Roberts, 25 November Buried in Norwood Cemetery, London

Egypt

The recorded history of Egypt is one of the longest known, although dates before 1500 BC are continually disputed. There were 30 Dynasties, or ages, and these are divided into three major periods — the Old, Middle and New Kingdoms — and several lesser periods. The Dynastic divisions were devised by Manetho, an historian priest writing during the reigns of the first two Ptolemies, not long before the birth of Christ.

Dynasties 1 and 2 (c.3100 BC – 2686 BC) are referred to as the Archaic period and very little is known of them, beyond the fact that Dynasty 1 was founded by the legendary Menes. He united the earlier kingdoms of Upper and Lower Egypt and traditionally is believed to have founded a new capital at Memphis.

The Old Kingdom is usually thought to begin with the 3rd Dynasty and end with the 6th. It was the period of major pyramid building and lasted from around 2686 BC to 2181 BC. The power of the king (or pharaoh), which was absolute, was at its height at this time but towards the end of the Dynasties of the Old Kingdom it began to disintegrate into feudal anarchy.

The 7th to the 10th Dynasties, known as the First Intermediate Period, was a time of Egyptian weakness, about which little is known beyond the fact that central admin-istration no longer functioned.

The Middle Kingdom (Dynasties 11 and 12, from around 2133 BC to 1786 BC) centred on Thebes to begin with, and was the classic period of ancient Egyptian art. Economic progress led to expansion abroad with expeditions being sent to Libya, Nubia and Sinai. Once again, however, the internal strength of the pharaohs declined and eventually most of Egypt was overrun by outsiders and the Second Intermediate Period began. It lasted for five Dynasties, the 13th to the 17th, and covered the years from around 1786 BC to 1567 BC.

The New Kingdom saw the establishment of a strong central government and comprised the 18th, 19th and 20th Dynasties. The Egyptian artistic revival began in the reign of Hatshepsut of the 18th Dynasty, and her successors contrived to strengthen Egypt's position as an expanding empire and a prosperous country.

After the New Kingdom, there was a series of Dynasties which ended with defeat for Egypt by the Persians, who founded the 27th Dynasty in 525 BC. The Persians remained the effective rulers of Egypt until they were driven out by Alexander the Great in 332 BC. Alexander appointed one of his generals, Ptolemy, as governor of Egypt and it was he who subsequently founded the Ptolemaic Dynasty which ruled Egypt for 300 years until defeated by the Romans in 30 BC.

A letter, dated 24 September, from Roberts to his daughter, gives his first impressions:

This morning we were all early astir, and Alexandria lay before us, its mosques and palm-trees giving it a different character from anything I had seen ... Our ship was soon surrounded by the most picturesque boatmen ... pulling, hauling and bawling — each fighting for which should have the passenger.

On entering the city we saw long trains of loaded camels and donkeys; Turks in rich dresses; negroes, some nude; with Greeks, Jews and people of all nations. Having taken up our abode we sallied forth to see the lions, visited the bazaars and the slave market ... The slaves were mostly girls: some from Circassia were well dressed; others, negroes, squatted on the ground, with scanty bits of matting thrown round them, and in a sun that would have killed a European. It was altogether a sickening sight, and I left it proud that I belonged to a nation who had abolished slavery.

Roberts's Journey in Egypt

The artist travelled nearly 1,000 miles from Alexandria to Abu Simbel.

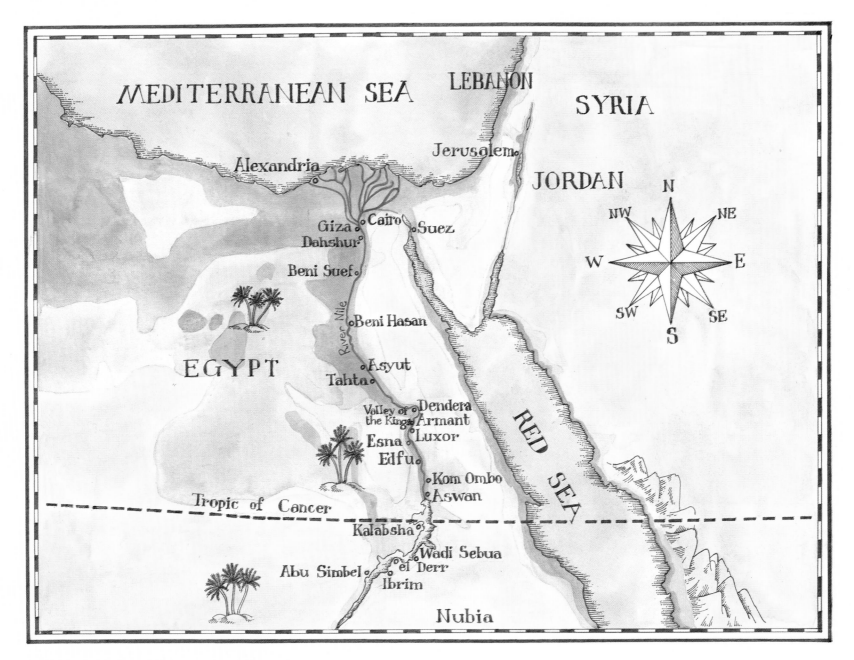

24-27 September

24 September

Monday 8 o'clock and in sight of Alexandria. There stands the fortress on the site of the ancient Pharos. The modern city is in the foreground but the ancient Alexandria is a mass of ruins more celebrated as the battle ground on which the French and English contended for what?

With Pompey's Pillar I must say I was disappointed. This could not be from its situation for it stands on a height and is seen to the greatest advantage. It is composed of 5 slabs — viz the pedestal, plinth, base, shaft and capital. There can be no doubt of its being surmounted by a statue, supposing it was not one of many belonging to a temple, a thing I think most probable from the appearance of the mound on which it stands.

A great part of the celebrated obelisk called Cleopatra's needle appears to be buried. … it is not improbable it may have stood on a pedestal — from one that is lying close to it and of the same dimensions … it must have formed the entrance to a temple.

25 September

Up at ½ past 5 and rode round the ancient town with Mr L — Found the remains of a Portico partly cleared out, consisting of six granite columns standing upright; the inside wall probably of a temple with rude painting of ornamental scroll work and a Roman soldier on horseback.

Hired a servant to go up the Nile, by name Ishmael, and gave orders for provisions for 4 months.

26 September

Made preparations for my journey and rode with Mr L to Cleopatra's baths and the catacombs … . I dined with the Consul General who is to give me an introduction to Mehemet Ali also an introduction to the mosques of Cairo.

27 September

After laying in all things necessary for 4 months voyage up the Nile we left Alexandria at 6 o'clock.

Far Left: Obelisk at Alexandria

Left: Pompey's Pillar

Today fewer travellers make their way to Egypt through Alexandria, and those who do find little of antiquity to impress them in this city which was once the site of the Pharos lighthouse, one of the Seven Wonders of the Ancient World. Named after Alexander the Great who founded it in 331 BC, it was the capital city of Egypt for over 1,000 years. The Pillar was mistakenly called after Pompey but in fact dates from 300 AD when it was built to honour the Emperor Diocletian who saved the city from famine. The two obelisks known as Cleopatra's Needles which were in Alexandria in Roberts's time were originally erected nearly 1,500 years before, in Heliopolis. They were removed to Alexandria in 10 BC after the defeat of Antony and Cleopatra.

28-30 September

28 September

This morning about 9 we arrived at the junction of the canal of Machmodi with the Nile, and here I first saw this celebrated river. The stream was very strong and thick as mud could make it. There is a considerable village here. We discharged our boat and took a fresh one of larger size between four of us … . We passed several villages on both sides of the river whilst the night closed in with the most beautiful moonlight. After smoking my shabouk I wrapt myself in my cloak and lay on the deck, if the bottom of the boat deserved such a name.

29 September

Up with the sun this morning and landed at a village on the right bank where there was an Arab fair, of which I think we were the greatest curiosities. They were pouring in from all quarters with cattle, goats, fowls, fruit, tobacco in the leaf and otherwise. The Nile here flows very rapidly, and the water is brown and thick; it is past its height and has fallen two feet. The country as far as the eye can see on either side is richly cultivated, and thickly interspersed with villages generally surrounded by palm trees, which combined with the minarets of the mosques form the most picturesque scenes. The mosques are white and the houses, which are merely hovels are of the mud of the Nile and were it not for their square form, would not be distinguishable from the earth by which they are surrounded.

30 September

Slept little last night being tormented with all the plagues of Egypt combined. We were hauled up all night, which is simply done by driving a stake into the ground, a rope from the ship is attached to this stake, & it being, to a great depth, a rich alluvial soil, it is easily driven. The whole of the country through which we have passed is richly cultivated, and here begins the sand hills to the right, which are driven into high mounds or hillocks, interpersed with maze grounds, the cotton plants and inumerous palm trees and many of the water wheels for irrigation. About half past 11 we first caught a glimpse of the Pyramids — what sensations rush upon us at first sight of these stupendous monuments of past ages. The mystery in which they have ever been enveloped, the very object of their erection wrapt in oblivion. What were the stupendous works of Roman art compared to these …

Pyramids of Giza from the Nile

Although the remains of more than 50 pyramids are scattered throughout Egypt, the three pyramids of Giza have always attracted the most attention because of their size and perfection of construction. They were probably robbed of their original contents in antiquity but the systematic excavation of the site began in the first half of the 19th century.

Napoleon calculated that it would be possible to build a wall around France with the stone from the Great Pyramid of Cheops alone.

The Mosque of Sultan Hassan

The Mosque of Sultan Hassan was built on a vast scale as a madrasa, or theological college, and work began on it in 1356. It was constructed of stone and it was planned that it should have four huge minarets. In fact, only three were built and one fell down in 1361, killing over 300 people. Another collapsed in 1659 and presumably this weakened the entire edifice because the huge dome fell in in 1660. Reconstruction by the Ottomans began in 1671, and the dome was restored in the 18th century. The remaining original minaret is the largest in Cairo.

The fountain which can be seen in Roberts's drawing is difficult to date precisely although its site is thought to be original. The date on it is that of the year in which construction of the Mosque was completed but it is possible that the Ottomans rebuilt the fountain incorporating a copy of the original inscription.

Hassan was elected sultan when he was only 12 or 13 years old. He faced a revolt around 1361 and was executed. Although his tomb is in the Mosque, it is not known if he was interred there. However, two of his sons were buried in the tomb chamber.

30 September – 1 October

30 September

About 4 o'clock we came in sight of Boulak — the port of Cairo and our ship drew up beside a boat filled with Negro slaves for sale: some of them perfect models in form ... After discharging the boatmen we hired donkeys and proceeded to Mesr-el-Kahira or Cairo. Boulak is a large suburb and the minaret of the mosque of the most picturesque imaginable. After proceeding along a raised road with grounds flooded on each side we entered the celebrated city which I found exactly what I had expected. Long streets narrow and crowded with projecting shops. We made our way to Hills the only English hotel here.

Kinnear includes a description of the hotel in his account of his journey called 'Cairo, Petra and Damascus in 1839':
I find nothing very English about the house, except the bills, which are extravagantly high, and the passengers to Suez, who in bad dinners, khamseen winds, prickly heat and fleas, have abundant opportunities of indulging their national privilege of grumbling.

1 October

This morning after calling upon the Consul, we hired donkeys and a Janissary and proceeded to view the town. The first thing of note is the mosque of Sultan Hassan and I was surprised and pleased with its magnitude, the beauty of its decorations and the costliness of the materials; but like every other mosque as well as the city itself it is fast falling into decay.

1 October

We then visited the Alcazar or Citadel, the view from which was to me the most novel and beautiful I had ever seen. Cairo with its numerous domes and minarets lay before me and the magnificent mosque of Sultan Hassan, beyond is the suburb of Boulak and the windings of the Nile and in the distance the Pyramids of Ghizeh with the chain of hills of Libya.

Cairo looking West

Saladin's Citadel is now crowned with the Mosque of Mehemet Ali which was begun in 1824 but not completed until 1857.

In 1811, Mehemet Ali invited nearly 500 Mameluke beys to a palace, formerly on the site of the Citadel. As they were about to leave, his troops opened fire. Tradition has it that one bey escaped when his horse leapt over the fortress wall and plunged nearly 60 feet. The horse died, the bey escaped but Mehemet Ali ensured that his position as ruler of Egypt was secure.

Roberts sketched this view of Cairo from the high mounds of rubbish which were piled outside the city walls. The view from the Citadel remains magnificent and the Pyramids are still visible today, despite modern building.

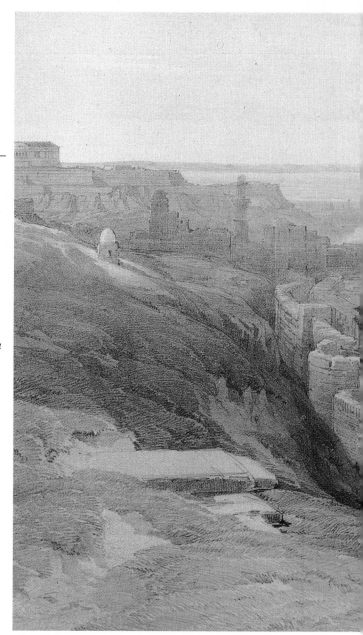

2-4 October

2 October

Made an agreement with the Captain of my boat for three months to ascend the Nile as high as the Second Cataract for which I am to pay £15 or 1300 Piastres per month.

3 October

Started for Ghizeh this morning to see the Pyramids ... . I was not so much struck with the enormous dimensions of the great Pyramid until I began to ascend it, which is an awful task. The Sphinx pleased me even more than the Pyramids.

4 October

Rode to Boulak to have my boat put under water. Bought a flag.

This boat was described in a letter as:

> ... a boat with a small cabin about six feet long by five broad and five feet six high. An Arab servant and myself completed complement, in seaman phrase. In order to clean the boat or drown the vermin with which it was infested I had it sunk in the Nile for a night.

Head of the Great Sphinx

The method of pyramid building developed between the 3rd and the 4th Dynasties with the transition from the construction of pyramids in the 'step' style (the Step pyramid at Saqqara is the most famous example and is thought to be the oldest building in the world) to the 'true' pyramid shape of the pyramids of Giza.

They were erected by three pharaohs of the 4th Dynasty; Cheops (Khufu), Chephren (Khafre) and Mycerinus (Menkaure). Chephren, the second pharaoh to build at Giza, erected his mortuary temple on the eastern side of his pyramid and this was linked by a causeway to the Valley temple. The Sphinx is situated just north of the causeway and was developed from a natural outcrop of rock.

The concept of the sphinx originated in Egypt and was adopted throughout the ancient world; representations can be found in Assyrian, Roman and Greek art. In Egypt, the head of the sphinx is usually in the form of a royal portrait while the strength of the pharaoh is represented by the body of a lion.

Throughout the centuries, shifting sand has repeatedly encroached upon the Sphinx, covering up the efforts made to expose it. Between its paws stands a commemorative stela which records how a young prince fell asleep in the shade of the statue and dreamed that he would become a pharaoh if he cleared away the sand — the prince became Tuthmosis IV who ruled from 1425 to 1417 BC, one thousand years after the construction of the Sphinx.

French engineers brought to Egypt by Napoleon began the modern excavation of the Sphinx and in 1816 the head was revealed. By the time of Roberts's visit, very little further work had been done and he would only have seen the head — which he greatly admired.

Chephren's Valley temple was only discovered by Mariette in 1852, despite its close proximity to the Sphinx. Mariette continued his excavation of the Valley temple throughout the 1860s but he did not attempt to clear the sand and debris from the Sphinx. Subsequent archaeologists, either through lack of time or money, also failed to excavate it and it was not until 1925 that any more serious work was undertaken.

It can now be seen more or less complete although the beard and part of the nose is missing. Fears of erosion to the soft stone continue, not only from sand but from the rising water-table.

5-7 October

5 October

Today visited the tombs of the Caliphs; like everything else here they are little better than ruins and inhabited by the poorest wretches, totally incapable of seeing or understanding the exquisite workmanship of which they are composed. A wretched tomb was erected in the midst of the most splendid dome; evidently built of the spoil of some other mausoleum. Nothing I have ever seen equals the beauty of the mosaic work of the floors and walls, which are principally inlaid with mother of pearl and precious stones.

6 October

Rode this morning with Mr N- to view several mosques at Cairo. In the afternoon we took our departure for Boulak. Captain N- & Mr V- in one boat and I in another. The wind being against us we lay too all night. In the morning still very little wind but rather more favourable, and we proceeded on our voyage.

7 October

Stung to death last night with the mosquitoes — could not bear the net owing to the closeness of the cabin, and so paid the penalty. Dined with my friends on board their boat. We passed the pyramids of Ghizeh & Dashour. Went to bed with my hands burning with the bites of not only mosquitoes, but I think of the large ants which are everywhere. Beautiful moonlight nearly all night.

Left: Tombs of the Caliphs

Regarded as one of the jewels of Islamic architecture, the mausoleum of Kait Bey, built in 1474, is the finest of the tombs of the Caliphs. Roberts's view shows how great was its state of disrepair in 1839, and its restoration did not begin until 1898. It is only in recent years that attention has been given to Cairo's wealth of Islamic monuments.

Right: View on Nile towards Pyramids of Dashur

The unusually shaped 'bent' pyramid of Dashur was a predecessor of the Giza pyramids and an architectural development from the Step pyramid of Saqqara.

8-9 October

8 October

Little or no wind today, rowed great part of the way ... . Beyond the fields, which extend very little way from the river is a long chain of hills to the left, covered with sand and without the slightest appearance of vegetation. On the right of the stream stood the celebrated Memphis but excepting the pyramids of Dashour it is impossible to distinguish any indication of buildings.

9 October

By 4 this afternoon only at Bibbe there being scarcely any wind. At Beni Souef there was a market or bazaar as they call it here; numerous groups of the country people flocked along the banks to the town; the women old and young were dressed alike in a blue cotton dress, open in front with hanging sleeves; and allmost all of these carried burdens on their heads of baskets of fruit, principally dates and melons, or pigeons of which great numbers appear to be reared here. The men with flocks of sheep or goats. The groups were very picturesque most of the women carrying children in the Egyptian fashion, on the left shoulder.

11 October

Having left in the middle of the night with a good wind I found myself at daybreak near a town on the left bank called Wady Metaghara and within an hours sail of the celebrated caves or catacombs of Beni Hassan, but who Beni Hassan was or what a modern saracenic name has to do with monuments of the ancient Egyptians, I cannot conceive. The rocks or hill containing the caves is a continuation of the long range of sand hills to be traced the whole way from Cairo, along the East bank of the river ... . The caves or apartments are in the face of the rock rising immediately above the left bank of the Nile, they are of a white sand-stone and are arranged in a line nearly on the same level. To the principal ones there seems to be a road or approach with large blocks of rough stones on either side. In front and cut in the rock is a sort of façade or Portico supported by two octagonal columns with a Doric plinth and above is an indication of a projecting cornice although it is not so distinctly visible in this as in others. If true that the paintings inside these apartments are 900 years previous to the Christian era, little doubt can be entertained as to the Greek Doric being derived from this ... . The walls are covered with the celebrated paintings copied by Champollion and others, showing the domestic arrangements and sports of the ancient Egyptians. They are painted in rows upon a white ground ... . All of these caves have wells or pits nearly all choked up though some of them seem to have been recently opened and from the appearance of some mummy clothes scattered about something of their kind must have been found ... . We were particularly struck by the beautiful panorama that lay beneath us. The Nile, here broad and winding and the plain covered with vegetation, but no trace of anything human was to be seen with the exception of our small craft which lay on the bank beneath. Those plains that had once teemed with the 'busy lives of men' were now little better than a vast wilderness — one or two deserted villages of mud lay along the banks beneath, but not a human being was to be seen.

Entrance to the Tombs of Beni Hasan

These tombs were cut out of the hillside for the local provincial governors during the reigns of the Middle Kingdom pharoahs of the 11th and 12th Dynasties. The interior decorations have deteriorated since Roberts's day and scholars now have to rely on copies made in the 19th century. One famous painting shows a Semitic tribe, dressed in brightly-coloured striped robes, entering Egypt at a border post. This was believed by some to depict Abraham and his tribe seeking refuge from famine, but the accompanying hieroglyphic texts describe them as traders from the Red Sea.

13-18 October

13 October

This morning, like all mornings here, lovely ... . At Siout. It is the see of a Coptic bishop, and is affirmed to be the place where the Virgin and Infant Saviour took refuge from their oppressor. It is said that many Copts, in this belief, come here to die. Some mounds of rubbish outside the town and a number of sepulchral excavations outside the town are the only remains of this ancient city ... . Upon entering the town the first object which presents itself is the large mosque with its lofty minaret of which I made a sketch. Last night Ishmael, my servant who sleeps outside my cabin, had all his clothes stolen even to his shoes.

16 October

We left Tahta early not a breath of wind ... . Having promised the boatmen, yesterday, that I would give them a sheep, we went ashore at Maragheh where there was a fair for the purpose of puchasing one ... . Being rather closely pressed whilst making our bargain we found we were surrounded by several armed Arabs, who gave us to understand that the Sheik or Governor wished to speak with us. They were two very fine looking men in the prime of life and elegantly dressed. Having made our salaam they begged us to be seated as the carpet was none of the largest. Our friend 'Pickwick', who is not altogether free of gout yet, was not a little put to it: his anxiety to comply with the customs, his difficulty in crossing his short fat legs, together with the dreadful thought of how he was to get up again, puzzled him sadly.

18 October

There is to me the gratification of being for the first time commander of a vessel with a crew of 8 or 9 men at my disposal. I now and then look up to the British ensign with no little degree of pride, as some vessel passes me with her tattered flag with its Arabic inscription or the Pasha's with its crescent and star ... . But we are now drawing near Dendyra the most beautiful of all the Egyptian temples, and I shall soon see whether all my hopes are to be realized.

Siout — Upper Egypt

An unusual view by Roberts in Upper Egypt showing only Islamic monuments and a passing camel train. So unused were the local population to itinerant artists that Roberts records he was mobbed here by a crowd.

19 October

By day break I was astir and accompanied by my friend Captain N- to the ruins, who greatly assisted me in taking the measurements .... The portico of the temple stands so high above the surrounding ruins that it is seen from the river. Upon entering it, I was struck with amazement first at the beautiful preservation in which I found every part, excepting where it had been purposely defaced which was the case with nearly all within reach: and secondly with the endless labour bestowed upon the carving, for here every part is literally covered with hieroglyphics from top to bottom and from roof to roof, outside as well as inside, even the narrow staircase where day light could not penetrate, from figures raised fifteen feet in height to those so small that they might be examined with a glass. This must have been the work of ages. Much must be buried in the rubbish that has accumulated round the temple. The first object that strikes you on your approach is a gateway much injured, but which must have originally been intended to be flanked with propylons. You then approach the Portico or inner temple and on coming near you are struck with the magnitude of the parts combining breadth with the most minute detail. There follows the temple itself with two chambers leading to the sanctuary or cella every part of which is covered and all have been painted outside as

well as in. Sufficient remains to restore in drawing nearly the whole: … . The day was spent in taking measurements and night was closing ere I left it … . As the setting sun gilded the high peaks of the Lybian chain and threw the broad shadow of the temple itself, across the plain, it was a scene that indeed called up the saddest reflections.

Far left and left: Temple of Dendera

The Temple of Hathor, the cow goddess, is one of the best preserved in Egypt. It was begun in the Ptolemaic period and completed by the Romans, about 60 AD.

In Roberts's drawings, he sometimes accurately left the faces of the goddesses blank on the capitals of the columns — these features had been either worn away or desecrated by squatters who had occupied the temple. The smoke from their fires had blackened the ceilings and much of the relief decoration was severely defaced by fanatical Copts.

21 October

Thank God we are approaching this most celebrated city. Here the French army made a dead pause and burst into one unanimous shout on beholding this field of ruins. This morning like all others here is delicious and we have a cool breeze from the north. Here the plain extends to a greater breadth than any part we have yet passed. To our left are seen the propylons of Karnac surrounded by palm trees over the tops of which I can distinguish two obelisks. Several guides have already surrounded the boats holding out rolls of paper, which I had at first taken for the papyrus but which we found to be recommendations from their last employers. They are a sad annoyance forcing themselves upon you and making more noise and disturbance than the little they can guide you to will compensate you for.

Karnac — General View from the Temple of Khonsu

Karnac is the largest of the monuments to be seen at ancient Thebes, modern Luxor. This was the capital of Egypt during the New Kingdom period, which began around 1567 BC and was the home and burial place of the pharaohs of the 18th, 19th and 20th Dynasties. The temples of Karnac and Luxor on the east bank were dedicated to Amun, king of the gods, whereas those on the west were the mortuary temples of the pharaohs themselves. Here they were venerated after death in the form of the god of the underworld, Osiris.

Amun is often referred to as the 'king of the gods' although in the Old Kingdom he was virtually unknown. During the Middle Kingdom period (c. 2050–1750 BC), Thebes and its god grew rapidly in importance. The pharaohs of the New Kingdom, with the one notable exception of Akhenaten, claimed to be sons of Amun and made additions to his temple at Karnac. Akhenaten broke away from this pattern, changed his name from Amenhotep, and founded an entirely new religion and capital city dedicated to the worship of the sun disk 'Aten'. The treasures of Amun were appropriated by the new god and the reliefs and inscriptions at Karnac were mutilated to remove the name of Amun. However, the new religion was shortlived and Akhenaten's successor changed his own name from Tutankhaten to the now famous one of Tutankhamun. After his restoration Amun was incorporated with the sun god Ra and as Amun-Ra became by far the most important of the Egyptian deities, and the pharaohs of the 19th Dynasty, in particular Ramesses II, built large additions to his temples. As with many of the Egyptian gods, Amun is associated with a wife and son to form a triad. Both the goddess Mut and her son Khonsu had their own temples within the Karnac complex.

With the death of Ramesses XI, last pharaoh of the 20th Dynasty in c. 1085 BC, the New Kingdom is regarded as at an end. Upper Egypt was ruled from Thebes by the High Priests of Amun as a virtually independent state. At the same time pharaohs ruled the north of the country from their capital of Tanis in the delta. The High Priests endeavoured to repair the damage done by tomb robbers to the burials of the New Kingdom pharaohs during the 20th Dynasty. They rewrapped those mummies that survived and placed them in a secret hiding place along with the mummies of the High Priests themselves. Here they remained undisturbed until forty years after Roberts's trip.

21 October

Having arrived at Gurna little time was lost in hiring donkeys and proceeding to view the ruins: crossing a field the first one came to were the remains of a small temple on the right in a state of great dilapidation.

Further on is the Memnomium in which I was rather disappointed as to the magnitude but was surprised at the masses of stone of which it is composed.

The proportions of the pillars of which there are two kinds is beautiful. The head and shoulders of the Memnon lying on the ground is enormous, one can only wonder how it got there. The trouble of dislodging it must have been almost equal to the erection. From the situation, it could not have been the effect of an earthquake and had this been the case not a pillar could have remained around it. A small head and body of the same figure in black basalt is very beautiful and has Belzoni's name marked on it: on the left is a huge propylon shattered to pieces with a huge battle scene sculptured upon it.

We next proceeded southwards to the celebrated statues on the plain; they are immense indeed, but insufficient remains to give an idea of what they have been.

We then came to the heaps uncovered by Mr Salt which was the temple to which these figures are supposed to have been the guardians.

Above: Fragments of the Colossi at the Memnomium

The mortuary temple of Ramesses II (1304–1237 BC), the Memnonium is situated on the west bank opposite Luxor. The collapsed statue described by Roberts was the largest ever carved by the Egyptians and weighs over 1,000 tons.

Belzoni removed a statue from the temple and it was the sight of this, exhibited at the British Museum in 1818, which inspired Shelley to write his sonnet 'Ozymandias'.

> *I met a traveller from an antique land*
> *Who said: Two vast and trunkless legs of stone*
> *Stand in the desert. Near them on the sand,*
> *Half sunk, a shatter'd visage lies …*

Right: Colossi of Memnon at the Inundation

These two statues once flanked the entrance to the mortuary temple of Amenhotep III of the 18th Dynasty. It was demolished by Ramesses II for use as a source of building material for his own monumental works. Since the building of the Aswan High Dam stopped the annual flooding, or inundation, of the fields of Egypt, this view of the statues has disappeared.

21 October

We next visited Medinet Habu which is of all on the west side the most extraordinary and beyond all description. After being there some hours I reluctantly left it to visit a very beautiful small temple in the hollow of the mountains with the Isis head pillars in the most exquisite taste. Inumerous dead bodies were lying about. By this time the sun was setting & we turned our asses heads to our boats. Upon our way back we found several Arabs standing in the road with mummies one of them very beautifully painted and numerous ornaments which they offered us for sale.

Left: Deir el Medinah

Built in Ptolemaic times, this small temple was used by artisans working on the royal tombs in the Valley of the Kings. Nearby are the ruins of 70 houses belonging to workmen and their families and their own tombs can also be seen, showing how much the artisans were influenced by their construction of royal tombs.

Above: Medinet Habu

This is the best preserved of the mortuary temples on the west bank and was built by the Pharaoh Ramesses III (1198–1166 BC). Contemporary accounts show that this temple was the focus of the economic and administrative life for the whole of Thebes for several hundred years after the death of Ramesses III.

The earliest recorded strike protest took place here in the reign of Ramesses III; tomb workers from Deir el Medinah resorted to demonstrations, perhaps because of shortage of rations.

22 October

I went by sunrise to Gourna and carefully examined the temple. After breakfast we set out for Beban el Malook, the tombs of the kings of Thebes. The road to it winds for about two miles into the mountains immediately behind the plain. I cannot imagine anything more grand than these ruins so totally unlike every thing of their kind: rocks towering over rocks while not a blade of grass or any vegetation whatever was to be seen.

The heat was intense. It brought to my mind the story of Aladdin, and the wild scene in the mountain with the magician. This was the very spot for such a scene and upon descending into the tomb called Belzoni's, I could not help thinking, the subsequent part of the story might have been realized.

This tomb has been so often described that I will not attempt it farther than to say that excepting destruction of its parts by C- and others it is in such a beautiful state of preservation that it appears the work of yesterday. If the hieroglyphics can be read surely here would be found the whole system of Egyptian mythology. Here is the whole pantheon drawn in such a masterly hand and in such endless variety that every system may here be seen as distinctly as when these temples were crowded with their notaries. This splendid mausoleum never having been finished you have here the whole process from the smoothing of the rock to the outline with red chalk, there follows a correcting hand with a black outline of size and colour and lastly the scooping out into the form.

We afterwards visited several others of which I am told there are twenty-two, but all in a state of greater dilapidation. We afterwards rode to Medinet Habu and to the sitting statues.

Entrance to the Tombs of the Kings of Thebes

Tuthmosis I was the first pharaoh to have his tomb cut in the cliffs of this valley. He had seen how the ancient pyramids of earlier pharaohs had been desecrated by tomb robbers and felt that secret burial was necessary in order to preserve his body and treasures for the afterlife. Many later pharaohs followed his example and over 60 burial chambers have been discovered; the tomb of Tutankhamun revealed in 1922 is, so far, the only chamber to have survived virtually intact.

Roberts visited the tomb of Seti I, considered to be the finest in the valley, which had been excavated by Belzoni in 1817. The pharaonic litany of death is wonderfully illustrated on the walls in bas-relief but the only material treasure which Belzoni discovered was an empty alabaster sarcophagus. He removed it and it is now in the Sir John Soane Museum in London.

22 October

On our return we found a set of dancing girls ready to receive us — after dinner we witnessed their performance. Much has been written of these girls peculiar to the East but nothing comes up to the real scene. The party consisted of six, one a very tall negress, of the five others three only were good dancers. One a black girl, elegant in person and equally graceful in her dancing, with one of the most expressive countenances I ever beheld. Nearly all of these have been banished to Esneh.

Dancing Girls

Roberts was less explicit in his account of the dancing girls than some of his contemporaries; perhaps his original report was censored, either by himself to spare his daughter's blushes, or by Christine when she copied out his Journal.

23 October

Luxor. This morning I walked over the vast remains of this mighty edifice, it is buried up with the mud houses of the modern town. The great propylon which faces the north is the first approached, it is in a tolerable state of preservation but half buried. Of the two obelisks which were at the entrance, one only remains, the other graces the Champs Elysees in Paris. The English are to have the other but it is to be hoped that they will let it remain where it is, for however interesting these may be to the antiquarian, they are out of place every where but surrounded by the temple which harmonizes with them. On each side of the gateway there are two colossal sitting figures buried up to the chest and sadly mauled like everything else that came within reach of the hammers.

Entering the gate and following my guide I clambered to the top of the propylon; where I could see the spacious remains of this once magnificent temple, clustered round it without order were the modern houses twisting out and in between the pillars the smaller of which are of a different form from those of the nave, if I may so term them, and appear partly over the wretched dwellings that cling round them not forgetting the mosque itself with its tiny minaret scarce reaching the top of the huge propylon; whilst the obelisk one entire stone soars above like the work of a divinity. It only wanted such contrasts as

these to prove the mighty works of ages long gone by, for in this country with the purity of its atmosphere and the long level plains upon which they stand, no notion can be formed of their magnitude until you approach very near them, and as is the case here it is only by contrasting them with the houses by which they are surrounded, that you can see the grandeur of them. The main pillars which are 30 feet in circumference may give some idea of the proportions; the capitals which are overspread in the form of the lotus must be about 50 feet in the outer circle. Every part of them is covered with carving and these painted in the most glowing colours of which much has retained its pristine purity. The whole building extends from the propylon to the waters edge where there are the remains of a quay which is called Roman.

<u>Above: Grand Entrance to the Temple of Luxor</u>

<u>Left: Temple of Luxor from the Nile</u>

The houses clinging to the temple in Roberts's day were cleared away in 1885, by Gaston Maspero, then Director of Antiquities. He excavated the temple and left only the whitewashed mosque of Abu el Hagag, perched on top of the temple high above the ancient ground level. The second obelisk, which in antiquity would have been sheathed in gold or electrum (an alloy of gold and silver), was left in place to grace the entrance.

23 October

From this we proceeded to Karnac. If Luxor struck me with its magnitude what shall I say of Karnac? Its grandeur cannot be imagined. Were I to write what I think it would be mere rhapsody. It is so far beyond everything I have ever seen that I can draw no comparison. Like all the other temples, on approaching it you are disappointed, and I cannot understand Denon's account of the French army stopping in amazement and clapping their hands in an ectasy of delight on their turning a corner of a mountain and coming in sight of it. Now the plain on which they stand is a dead level to such an extent that they could be distinguished and that is all. It is only on coming near that you are overwhelmed as it were with astonishment: you must be under them and look up and walk around them and for this reason I am fearful, painting will scarcely convey any notion of what I mean.

The circumference of the main pillars are thirty-three feet six inches so that a man beside them appears as a pigmy. The stones overturned and lying around in every direction are so enormous that without considering the mode of their construction you are at a loss to conceive how they have been dislodged. One thing though is evident, more especially in this edifice, that the principal destruction has been caused by fire: in the closer passages and the entrance to the principal corridors the stones are splintered in every direction while perhaps those by it still retain their original beauty. The same thing may be seen at Dendyra and Medinet Habu where the Arabs have lighted their fires against the walls. The first object that strikes you is a large gateway.

Left: Ruins of Luxor from the Southwest

The 'shaduf' seen in the foreground is an ancient method of irrigation still in use today — water is raised with a counter-balanced lever-arm.

Right: Great Gateway leading to Karnac

The modern visitor to Karnac does not enter through this gate which dates from Ptolemy III. Beyond is the small temple of Khonsu, who was the moon-god son of Amun.

Great Gateway, leading to the Temple of Karnac—Thebes

David Roberts, R.A.
L. Haghe, lith.

23 October

Between the propylons is the main entrance to a spacious quadrangle in which is left one solitary column ... surrounding the whole of this is a colonnade of smaller pillars from which branch off cloisters supported also by colossal figures with their arms crossed on their breasts and holding the scourge and crook.

Crossing the court (or rather part of the temple for from the columns lying around it must have been covered like the rest) are two more propylons with a gateway between them the entrance of the great temple itself. This gateway is choked up with huge fragments of the roof and on the right hand is a multilated upright figure of Memnon. Beyond these columns are gateways seen through gateways, and obelisks, the most stupendous of the kind in existence. These pillars are 33.6 inches in circumference and on each side are rows of columns much lower forming aisles. Beside the greater these pillars suffer in apparent size but seen anywhere alone they would be colossal. The plinths of the capitals are 3 feet 6. This is so choked with its own ruin that it is difficult at first sight to know its exact form. The gateway beyond this is quite blocked up. Outside stands an obelisk with the remains of the corresponding one near it, and again an entrance of propylons of polished granite, and a 2nd obelisk. I should think the finest

in the world, without flaw and the polish as perfect as if the workmen had just left it.

The temple is continued still further on, pillar on pillar succeed each other. Extricating myself from them I now took the outer walls and found here a history to trace which would have taken days: processions and battles without number. Every thing is covered with carving and some of the most beautiful kind.

After viewing the two gates and the remains of the smaller temple we bade adieu to Karnac and at 5 o'clock got under weigh for Esneh and Nubia.

Far left: Karnac

Left: Great Hypostyle Hall

Karnac's history is long and complex, involving a progression from a simple local shrine to the greatest temple in Egypt during the New Kingdom. The complex comprises numerous small temples and shrines, with every pharaoh wishing to leave his mark on the temple of Amun. The relief work often shows signs of alteration, sometimes even obliterating the names of early pharaohs.

The city of Thebes began to decline towards the end of the New Kingdom when Ramesses II moved his capital to the delta and, despite periods of resurgence, it never regained its former glory. The town was destroyed by Assyrian invaders in the seventh century BC, but Alexander the Great and the Ptolemies made additions to the temples at Luxor and Karnac, 1,000 years after the height of their power.

The town rebelled against the Romans and was destroyed once more, leaving only a cluster of small villages. The early Christians converted the Luxor temple into a church and the Muslims erected a mosque on top of the temple to their saint Abu el Hagag, who was believed to have brought the 'True Faith' into Egypt.

Roberts was obviously fascinated by the magnitude of the columns of the Hypostyle Hall and many of his sketches depict them from different angles. The toppled stones have now been restored to show their grandeur and magnificence.

24 October

This morning at 7 I went ashore and visited the ruins of Hermonthis on the right bank about ½ a mile from the bank. These ruins, with the exception of Karnac and Luxor, are more picturesque than any I have seen. The temple is small and one part of it much encumbered with houses; the pronaos is unroofed, and the pillars stand by themselves. Near it is cleared out the foundations of a temple … . On the walls of the cella are hieroglyphics but sadly blackened; the principle objects are a line of cats, serpents and monkeys and the outside is also carved. Around the ruins are as usual immense mounds of earth covered with fragments of pottery and in the external parts are the remains of walls of unbaked brick. Here as everywhere else are herds of ferocious dogs which render it almost dangerous to pass.

Esneh — ancient Latopolis. On landing we proceeded to view the temple but found it covered with the houses of the town; after some little delay we got access to it. It is now used as a powder magazine, the walls are black and covered with the usual deities. The pillars are large and of the lotus form but from the care we had to take of our light it was nigh to impossible to see anything. After a stroll through the town and viewing one of the Pasha's cotton mills, which is now idle although at one time it employed 500 people, we returned to our boats.

On his return northwards on 25 November Roberts stopped to sketch the temple and recorded in his journal:

Whilst making my drawing I was nearly killed with kindness by the friendly Copts or Christians of this place — they seemed to consider me one of themselves and took every means of endeavouring to make me understand them. First by asking in Arabic and then in Greek both of which I am sorry to say are dead languages to me. At last a boy … drew a figure of a man holding a cross and on my making the sign of the same they seemed delighted … . I introduced a group of them in my sketch with which they seemed greatly pleased.

Above: Temple at Hermont

The temple, dedicated to the war god Montu, dated mainly from the time of the Ptolemies. It was dismantled not many years after Roberts had drawn it and the stones were used to build a sugar refinery.

Right: Temple at Esneh

This Ptolemaic temple dedicated to Khnum is now about 30 feet below street level as a result of the accumulation of rubbish and silt.

David Roberts R.A. [Edinburgh]

Portico of the Temple Edfou, Upper Egypt. Nov 25th 1838

26 October

This morning Captain N- and I landed at a village and walked about 5 miles across the country to Edfou. Walking at the rate of 4 miles an hour; we found the sun extremely hot. Between us and the river were fields of Indian corn ... and on our right the sands approach in some places close to the cultivated fields .... Midway was a Sheik's tomb in which were placed jars of water for a thirsty traveller. A lean hungry dog and two immense white eagles were gorging themselves on a dead camel and they scarely refrained from their repast upon our approach. Indeed birds of all kinds here seem scarcely to have any fear of man. The two propylons of the great temple were in sight the whole way and appeared as if placed on a height; this is solely owing to their size and to the smallness of everything around them, but the palm trees. Their height is about 100 feet. On entering the village and winding our way through the wretched hovels by which it is blocked up ... I stood in front of the most beautiful temple in Egypt. True it is not of the magnitude of Karnac nor is it in such preservation as Dendyra but it has all that these want. In every situation in which it is viewed it is a picture. It has breadth in its parts. The pillars are large massy and in form exquisite. Though half buried it is more beautiful than if laid open and reminds me of the Piranesi

etchings of the Forum of Rome .... I should think that next to Dendyra, this, if it were cleared out, would be found the most complete but the rubbish is up to the bottom of the capitals of the pronaos and the whole of the interior of the temple is buried. The façade or portico of the pronaos is the most exquisite in form I have ever seen, and every capital being different does not take from its beauty but in my opinion rather enhances it. ... At three we got on board our vessel and set sail but with very little wind.

On his return northwards on 23 November Roberts lingered at length in order to sketch the temple:

I made two large drawings of the portico and from it looking across the Dromos towards the propylons. To do the first I was

compelled to sit with my umbrella in the sun which today must have been 100 in the shade. I fear I did very wrong. I hope in God there may be no bad effects from it but the portico is so beautiful in itself I could not resist it. I now find my umbrella tent is little protection but for the future I shall avoid the sun even if I lose a subject.

Left: Portico of Temple of Edfu

Above: Temple of Edfu

The Frenchman Auguste Mariette, first Director of Antiquities, excavated this Ptolemaic temple dedicated to the hawk god Horus, in the 1860s. He revealed, as Roberts predicted, the most complete of Egypt's temples. Sadly, the original colours of the reliefs have long since faded but the unusual exploitation of light and darkness in the inner part of the temple must have greatly enhanced their richness.

27-28 October

27 October

Today there is scarcely a breath of wind. The crocodiles lye sunning themselves upon the bank, in the most perfect security, the cooing of the wild pigeons is heard close by in a grove of palm trees and the solitary crane stalks along by the river; whilst numerous birds are making the woods ring with their notes. Will this quiet place ever again become 'the busy haunt of men'? Nothing is more probable. Egypt is the medium of a recent intercourse with India and may not the flame of Christianity be rekindled along these shores, without its bigotry and intolerance?

In the course of the day whilst at anchor or stake Mehemet Ali passed us in a steamer on his way to the southern part of his dominions … . We heard at first indistinctly and then nearer and nearer the short rapid beat of the paddles. All on board were instantly in motion. There could be no doubt of it being the Pasha: everyone was in suspense, many of our boatmen never having seen a steamer. It was proposed that as is was the first steamer that has ascended the Nile, we should give them three hearty cheers after the English fashion, accordingly as they came abreast they were hailed with the hip hip hurra! … Immediately after, the alarm was given that the steamer was on the return

… . All was confusion, P- doffed his nightcap for his hat while our gallant friend was squeezing himself into a pair of military boots and wishing he could mount his regimentals. 'Bring my sword case' cried the Captain while P- was as eager in his demands for his card case and spectacles. I suggested the propriety of putting off and paying our respects: but it was only by sheer compulsion that we could induce the men to unmoor the boat and row to the middle of the stream, such is the terror his very name seems to inspire.

Roberts and his companions finally boarded the Pasha's steamer and conversed with the engineer — 'a worthy Scot'. Apparently the three cheers had greatly alarmed everyone on board but Roberts placated the crew and the steamer set sail again. Roberts and his friends beat a hasty retreat, without meeting the Pasha under whose protection they were travelling.

28 October

We reached about 9 o'clock Koum-Ombo. The approach to the temple is finer than any I have yet witnessed on the banks of the Nile. It stands upon a gentle height and when the temple of Isis was in existence must have had a most imposing effect, especially in coming down the river. The river which has gradually been encroaching on this part of the shore has swept away at least one temple if not more. The end of one propylon or rather gateway similar to that of Karnac is the only part left standing … . The colours of the winged globe, the invariable decoration of the roof, are still in excellent preservation. There are one or two capitals with the head of Isis as at Dendyra, but not mutilated … . Here too I found the cast skin of a serpent measuring about 4 feet. … I viewed it on all sides and each seemed better than another. It stands buried half way in the sands of the desert … . A few of the houses peeping above the sand which has drifted in from the desert is all that can be seen of the once proud city of Ombos. Like its rival Dendyra it is now a desolate wilderness, the haunt of the fox and the jackal, the serpent and the lizard.

Kom Ombo

The setting for the temple at Kom Ombo remains impressive and it is unusual because of its dual dedication — to the hawk-headed Horus and Sobek, the crocodile god. Its Ptolemaic columns have retained their rich colour and fine carvings, revealed to a much greater extent in 1893 long after Roberts's visit, when the sand and debris was cleared away.

Before the building of the first Aswan Dam crocodiles were a common sight in Egypt.

29 October

Syene or Es-Souan. We walked over the ruins of the ancient city which crown the height of a rock jutting out into the stream, a corresponding one being on the island of Elephantine opposite. The remains of a high Roman wall flank the rocks on that side and on the rock from which this rises as well as on the land side are hieroglyphics. Nothing remains of the ancient town but the brick walls and also the city walls. I examined the latter minutely but could find no remains of stone buildings. We walked through the modern town which has a paltry minaret rising in the midst of it shapeless and ugly. After breakfasting and making a drawing of this part of the river we crossed to the island of Elephantine. With the exception of the rubbish of the old town & a few columns no vestiges of its ancient temples are to be found. I saw one solitary figure with the arms folded on the breast holding flagilum and crook, and on examining the giant walls next the stream I found it composed of stones with hieroglyphics, which must have formerly belonged to some temple. We walked round the island but every part is equally destitute of ruins. The women appeared all occupied in making baskets. ...

Recrossing we went to see a collection of slaves from Nubia, which is indeed a most melancholy sight. They were principally boys and young women who appeared ill and sickly. Two were lying in a field evidently in the last stage of consumption. The men who were with them were good looking Nubians with the exception of one brutal looking fellow quite intoxicated, a most rare thing to see in this country. He was not black but his looks were equal to anything which the imagination could produce ... . The steamer ascended the cataract yesterday and all hands that could be procured were pressed into the service, one had therefore to wait all day for men and a pilot; night came on and they did not return; but we heard that they had such difficulty in taking her up that she was much injured and that the pilot had his arm broken. During the short time the Pasha was here yesterday he found time to hang one unfortunate fellow, though from what we have heard he seems to have richly deserved it.

Aswan and the Island of Elephantine

Aswan has a pleasant climate and its picturesque setting has made it a popular winter resort. The construction of the High Dam has restored its status as one of the principal cities of Egypt; in antiquity it was a border trading town through which gold, silver and exotic animals were transported into Egypt. Many statues and obelisks of the New Kingdom were hewn from granite quarried around Aswan.

30 October

This morning, finding there was no chance of ascending the cataract, Captain N- and I hired donkies and started for the place where we thought we were most likely to find the steamer lying. Having crossed the town our route lay through a long line of tombs which were scattered amidst the large granite rocks; some of them were covered with hieroglyphics, so that in all probability the place was used for the same purpose by the ancient Egyptians. A high ridge of rocks lay between us and the Nile, with here and there the tomb of some saint: all around was sterile and barren, not a green shrub enlivened the scene whilst the view was bounded on all sides by masses of shapeless and naked rock. After riding a little more than an hour, the view began to open and the palm and acacia were seen peeping from amongst the rocks, but beyond these were others more stupendous and bare and their black appearance so different from the light red sandstone we had become accustomed to, made them seem still more desolate. After riding for some time near the bank of the Nile we suddenly came in sight of the little island of Philae, a paradise in the midst of desolation. Its ruins even at a distance are more picturesque than any I have seen, perhaps this may be owing to the high barren rocks by which it is surrounded. To me it brought recollections of 'my father land' by reminding me of the first descent upon Roslin castle; why or wherefore I can scarcely tell, there is perhaps little similarity but there was sufficient to bring back the thoughts of my native land and the happy days of my youth. After hearing that the Pasha had proceeded on his voyage in a smaller boat and that the steamer had returned to Es-Souan to be repaired, we crossed over to the island of Philae in which I was much interested from the beauty of the remains with which I knew it abounded. The whole of the intermediate space that is not covered with the remains of the temple is strewn with the debris of the former town through which we scrambled our way with some difficulty to a square temple on the south of the island. It is in an unfinished state having the lotus formed capitals. The whole is as if the masons and carvers had but just left their employment; it is of a light sandstone and so sharp and beautiful in the detail that I could scarcely imagine that I was looking at a ruin of two thousand years standing ... . The whole is encumbered with the ruins of the mud huts with which every part of it has been covered even to the roofs of the temple ... . The colouring of the dresses of the various deities are so distinct that a correct representation could be given of the dress worn by each ... . On entering the great temple I was astonished and delighted with the elegant proportions ...

Philae — General View

After crossing the first cataract, travellers in 19th century Egypt arrived at the island of Philae, whose lushness made it the most romantic tourist attraction in the area. When the first Aswan Dam was opened in 1902, Philae was semi-submerged and its beautiful Ptolemaic temple of Isis was accessible only by boat when the water level was low. The construction of the High Dam in the 1960s meant that Philae would be permanently under water. An enormous project was undertaken to remove the temples and reconstruct them stone by stone on a neighbouring island. Here they can be seen today.

31 October - 1 November

31 October

This morning the steamer was brought back without her rudder and otherwise much injured. I was standing on the shore when she arrived and the Bey who had commanded her came up to me and invited me to his tent. Captain N- and I accepted his invitation and immediately repaired to his tent where we were served with coffee and pipes. He told us that the Pasha had given him orders to assist us in every way in his power ... . Having made arrangements for bringing our boats up I was anxious to get on and started for Philae. Our goods were landed at the village of Birbe opposite and on crossing we found that the boats were stuck fast half way for want of men and I had great difficulty in getting the luggage carried to where they were lying, which was by an island in the midst of the rapids. I found my men were afraid to trust themselves in a boat, so made up my mind to sleep with them where we were which was beside an encampment of boatmen who were gathering dates. It was beautiful moonlight and the night delicious. I wanted for nothing, having for food a few dates and plenty of Nile water. I had lighted my cigar and wrapped myself in my cloak for the night when we were agreeably surprised by the appearance of the men who were to take my boat up. They had

heard of our situation and had come to take us to our boat. Having got the luggage aboard we now ascended the stream which is here grand.

1 November

Today we had the treat of getting our boats through the rapids. They were unloaded and then rowed up by about 60 men of all ages and sizes. It was accompanied by great shouting and bawling which appeared indispensible here, but they safely towed us through with great difficulty ... . I made a large sketch of the temple called 'Pharoah's Bed' which seen in every direction is beautiful. The surrounding country is most extraordinary & unlike anything else: immense rocks peeping occasionally through the drifted sand, which as the night closed in had the appearance of snow; with here and there patches or strips of vegetation and close to the water's edge groups of palm trees. Having passed the rapids we entered Ethiopia and came to anchor just at sunset.

Above: Under the Grand Portico, Philae

While the temple was semi-submerged after the building of the first Aswan Dam, the visitor had to pass through the gateways in a boat.

Right: Philae — Pharaoh's Bed

Built in the reign of the Roman Emperor Trajan (98–117AD), this small but picturesque monument was originally intended as the entrance to the temples on the island of Philae.

2-3 November

2 November

The country hitherto above Philae has assumed a very different appearance from that of Lower Egypt; the hills and rocks are of a dark colour and from the river have all the effect of my native hills, they are sterile & barren but at a distance they do not appear so, whilst the banks and valleys abound with the domm and date palm, the fig and acacia trees, every patch of soil is covered with vegetation & the banks, where the Nile has overflowed are perfect gardens.

3 November

By breakfast time this morning we reached Kalabsha a village on the West bank, containing a magnificent temple the approach to which is from a landing formed of immense square stones close to the water's edge; stretching from this to a higher platform in front of the propylon which flanks the grand entrance, is a handsome terrace with parapet walls also of large square stones. The platform in front being higher it is approached by a slight ascent something between an inclined plane and step. Over the gateway is the winged globe and on the architrave of the door are symbolical figures. The walls of the two propylons are quite plain as are also the whole of the external walls with the exception of that at the back which contains large whole height figures ...

Passing under the portico or rather scrambling, for the door & interior are filled up with the large blocks originally forming the roof, we come to the pronaos which has formerly been supported by four columns only two of which survive. Beyond this is the cella also blocked up by the huge fragments of the roof. The walls are covered with carvings of the deities. They have been originally covered with clay and where this has rubbed off the colours are very fresh, but certainly not in such fine preservation as those of Philae ... . Two narrow flights of steps led from this to the top of the portico but the roof had fallen in & the remaining portion of the slabs that covered it were still suspended & by throwing forward the cornices rendered it dangerous to pass. I attempted to reach the propylon but could not succeed.

Winding our way through the village built close under the walls & in which I found a small column with Roman letters, we ascended the mountain to a small temple hewn in the rock ... . On each side of the entrance are the carving which has been so often described. We saw from the remains of the stucco on them that they had been taken off in plaster ... . The sculpture on the walls is beautiful in execution or rather in drawing. A figure holding another by a tuft on the crown of the head and brandishing a hatchet over him is not only well drawn but the African countenance of the vanquished contrasted with the fine Jewish looking head of the conqueror is superior to most things of the kind I have met with. It is said to be very old, if so art must have been on the decline long before the final extinction of the Egyptian hierarchy.

Temple of Kalabsha

This large temple is dedicated to the Nubian god, Mandulis, and, although on the site of a New Kingdom temple, it was mainly constructed by the Ptolemies and then rebuilt in the reign of Augustus.

It, too, was almost permanently under water from the beginning of this century, and so in 1962–63 West German experts removed its 13,000 blocks to a safe site adjacent to the High Dam.

The clay covering the walls to which Roberts refers was often applied by later inhabitants of the building who wished to cover up the carvings.

Early archaeologists frequently made plaster copies of reliefs and the marks of their work remained in evidence throughout the last century.

Amelia Edwards, an early pioneer of British Egyptology, sailed up the Nile in 1874 and tinted with coffee the remains of plaster sticking to the façade of Abu Simbel, in order to improve its appearance. Amelia Edwards later founded the Egypt Exploration Society.

3-5 November

3 November

It is four weeks tonight since I left Cairo. Good health in such a delightful climate, & the continual excitement of seeing new scenes has kept me from wearying. We are now approaching the termination of our voyage: No painter could do justice to the people here: today I met an Arab armed & mounted on his dromedary. He stood until I made a sketch of him and for the first time I regretted I had no bucksheys. He was a perfect picture, mounted on his white dromedary with its trappings, his spear & broadsword & his buckler slung by his side: his belt held a pair of silver mounted pistols. He seemed delighted & had a fine intelligent countenance; indeed the people improve every mile. All are armed; the knife is generally buckled to the arm or to the girdle and they carry the spear in the hand.

Later in his journey, on 16 November, Roberts encountered other Nubians:

I passed through several villages, the black inmates of which turned out on the whole line of route, but it seems that they must occasionally see travellers, as several of them came towards me with things to sell. I bought a dozen or so of small copper coins principally Roman, and of an Arab I bought his sword, a long broad one like a highlander's, a short one which hangs at his girdle, a charm which was strung to his left arm, his buckler made of the hide of the hippopotamus and a water bottle slung in a leathern pouch which was decorated with shells like the hair of their black beauties; for which I paid 141 piastres, about equal to £1 10s English money. At one cottage I made a sketch of a girl but not without great difficulty even with the promise of bucksheys they will scarcely consent to it.

4 November

We found ourselves at the upper part of the island of Derar above which on the West bank is a small temple. This island with the land on either shore is well cultivated, and the high rocky hills which have hitherto hemmed in the land, extending in some places to the water's edge, here entirely disappear. The sun has just risen and the effect is splendid over the white sands in the midst of which is the small ruined temple of Offalina with the dark purple hills partially seen in the distance. Here and there is a narrow strip of green or a group of palm trees reflected in the broad silent water of the Nile. Altogether it is a scene that forcibly reminds us how far we are from home yet one that the mind and eye loves to dwell upon.

5 November

No wind all day and the heat intolerable, P-'s thermometer 96 degrees in the shade, but it appears much more. After nightfall a light breeze sprang up from the north, and we made up a little for the loss during the day. The setting sun this evening was truly African. The burning appearance of the clouds reflected as they were in the river, with the long line of sands drifted in some places half way up the sides of the naked mountains, and the opposite height crowned with the desolate ruins of the ancient town formed a scene that would have delighted Turner. Long before the moon rose, we had our sails set to the light evening breeze and I sat till late on the deck reading the 'History of the Crusades' and enjoying the delicious coolness of the evening.

Group of Nubians

In the Late Period of Pharaonic history, the Nubian people turned the tables on their northern neighbour by conquering Egypt and ruling as the 25th of Manetho's Dynasties. They attempted to re-establish the glories of the New Kingdom age but were driven back south by an Assyrian invasion in 663 BC.

6-7 November

6 November

In the morning I found myself within a short distance of Wady Seboua. Here for many miles the sand of the Lybian desert has come quite to the water's edge, and there are no vestiges of vegetation except the acacia with its beautiful yellow blossoms, and along the surface of the sand was a prickly plant bearing a small pumpkin; there is also a beautiful green shrub which bears long green apples which upon opening we found were merely blown up with air; the stalk and long broad leaves emit a rich white pulpy milk which the Arabs say will blister the skin if touched by it. About a hundred yards from the bank of the stream are the remains of a temple with the two propylons facing the East, the back part of it including the pronaos is buried in the sand which is here drifted to a great depth, judging from the accumulation round the temple. To some distance round and mixed with the sand are the scattered fragments of pottery, the only remains of the former city, the name of which is not even known. Not a single habitation is seen around the smooth surface of the yellow sand unbroken save by the trail of the serpent or the tiny footsteps of the lizard; so completely have the words of the prophet been fulfilled, 'I will make the land of Egypt utterly waste and desolate, from Migdol to Syene, even unto the border of Ethiopia'.

About two hundred feet in advance of the propylons of the temple are two colossal figures also facing the East … . They are much corroded by time and otherwise much injured particularly the faces … . In a line with them and succeeded by others are two rows of sphinxes; two of these which are partly uncovered have the heads only above the sand … . Today the heat is excessive; no wind and the thermometer in the sun 115, & in the shade 98.

7 November

This morning found us a little below the town of Korosko on the eastern bank. The whole line of the western shore is still a desert, the sands being driven to the water's edge, skirted where it meets the water by a line of acacias. On the eastern shore the rocks almost approach to the river in many places terminating in it, here and there detached patches of verdure and a few palm trees are the only traces of vegetation.

I had noticed for some time an addition to our crew & I found upon enquiry that they had gone to the village beyond Korosko, & seized upon the first half dozen they could lay hands upon. Upon my asking the Reis what they were allowed, I was told by my servant that this is the usual way when a captain may want hands … . However it did not end here for shortly after passing the village our boat was surrounded by a band of these black savages, principally women screaming and yelling … . After much screaming and gesticulation on both sides, I jumped ashore, & with some difficulty learned that an old woman accused two of our sailors of having gone into her hut and stolen two dollars & a letter … . There is little doubt that the poor woman was robbed, but I think not by our men … . My servant who is very excitable seemed to look on the skirmish with the greatest coolness and was quite indignant when I offered to give the old woman something to put a stop to the affair.

Approach to Temple of Wady Sebua

This temple was one of several built by Ramesses II during his long reign from 1304–1237 BC. It was at one stage converted into a Coptic church.

From 1960, when the building of the Aswan Dam began, a massive archaeological campaign under the auspices of UNESCO set out to record the ancient sites which would be destroyed by the waters of Lake Nasser and, where possible, to move the temples to safety. The Sebua temple was moved some 2½ miles, but other temples were presented to foreign governments and travelled much greater distances.

8 November

We passed Derr in the early part of the night, & in the morning found we had been lying for some time near the village of Kette, in the territory of Wady Ibrim. The West shore continues to present the same desolate appearance, the sand extending to the water's edge bordered only by a few acacias; there are no villages, no palm trees, here and there may be distinguished the ruins of the sun dried brick of mud buildings. The East shore on the contrary appears well cultivated … . About 8 this morning we passed a large fertile island entirely cultivated with fields of Durra. Beyond this groups of palm trees begin to be seen on the west bank & here and there hamlets with their patches of wheat, on the left the rocks approach to the water's edge, and are a great height; on the ridge of one of them are the ruins of the ancient town and fortress of Ibrim. This, with the exception of the ancient temples is the only thing I have met with since leaving Cairo that has any appearance of durability; all the towns along the Nile are built of the plain mud of the river, or it is formed into bricks dried in the sun … . This fortress on the contrary approaches more in appearance to those of the Moslems which I have seen in Spain, both in situation & regularity of form, being built on the very brink of the precipice, and flanked at intervals with square towers of hewn or square stones. The whole is in a

most ruinous condition and I believe totally deserted.

The breeze being favourable we continued our course and I deferred any visit to it till my return. We are in hopes of reaching the termination of our long voyage tonight, Ibsambal, or as the natives call it Aboosemble. The western shore has resumed its former appearance, sand to the water's edge, whilst along the eastern the cultivation is carried on, the shore lined with palm trees, and occasional villages, in the background rise high naked mountains of a conical shape, but when mellowed by distance they are very beautiful, some of them might be taken for pyramids from the strata having the appearance of the layers of stone.

At last we have arrived all safe at Aboosemble.

Above: Approach to the Fortress of Ibrim

The fortress of Kasr Ibrim ceased to be manned only a few years before Roberts's arrival, when Mehemet Ali's conquest of Sudan had pushed the border further south. The foundations of the fort date from New Kingdom times, though during the Middle Kingdom it would no doubt have been one of a series of forts controlling this strategic site between the first and second cataract.

Right: Great Temple of Abu Simbel

Abu Simbel is by far the most impressive of Ramesses II's rock cut temples in Nubia. First reported by J.L. Burckhardt in 1813, it was opened by Belzoni in 1817 and obviously much visited by travellers in the following 20 years in view of the graffiti which horrified Roberts. Its spectacular façade consists of four colossal seated statues of Ramesses II which are about 68 feet high. Both the Great Temple and the smaller Temple were relocated between 1964 and 1968 to save them from the rising waters of Lake Nasser.

The Great Temple of Aboo simbel, Nubia

David Roberts, R.A.

Interior of the Temple of Abu Simbel

9 November

This morning the wind being favourable our friends left for the 2nd Cataract. By daybreak I was in the celebrated temple. They are on the face of the rock overhanging the river, the first or more northern is probably the most ancient but the one laid open by the indefatigable Belzoni is the most extraordinary. It faces the south east; the sand here pours down from the desert behind, so much that the three figures forming the façade are much buried. It having been described repeatedly I shall only give an outline of it.

There are four colossal figures cut out of the face of the rock in a sitting position like the celebrated Memnons on the plain of Thebes … . There is this difference however, these are in the most perfect condition while those at Thebes are much mutilated. Their preservation is owing to their having been buried in the sands so long accumulating round them, and it is almost to be wished that they were covered again for what with cockney tourists and yankee travellers, they stand every chance of being in a few years in a worse state. Is it not shocking to see these glorious specimens of art, the most ancient in the world, not only destroyed by relic hunters but carved with such names as Tomkins, Smith and Hopkins? The hand of the best preserved figure is completely destroyed, nothing being so delightful to these vermin as a finger or thumb or the great toe of a statue, & after committing such depredations they have the effrontery to smear their stupid names on the very forehead of the god. This is said to be the oldest of the Egyptian temples, if so, in what a labyrinth does it involve the whole history of these stupendous edifices. The beauty of the workmanship and its colossal dimensions are not to be surpassed by any other of the kind even at Thebes. If we compare it with the head of Isis on the temple of Dendyra the most elaborate and finished of all the Egyptian temples, Isis is barbarism itself, and yet Dendyra was the most recent. In this case the arts must have descended from Ethiopia into the fertile Egypt. If the key to the sacred language is really found, there can be little doubt from the excellent preservation of these monuments that we shall have the history of them.

The benign and placid expression of the countenance of these figures is only equalled by that of the Memnon in the British Museum, which must have been contemporary.

Interior of Temple of Abu Simbel

The Hypostyle Hall of the temple was cut deep into natural rock and the four statues of Ramesses II stand 30 feet high, in front of rock-cut pillars.

When the temple was re-sited, the reconstruction was perfect except for one thing; Ramesses II had built the temple to ensure that twice a year, on 21 February and 21 October, the rays of the rising sun would shine on his statue 205 feet deep in the sanctuary of the mountain temple. Modern engineers were not able to emulate their Egyptian predecessors so precisely and now the sun lights up the statue of the great pharaoh for 25 minutes twice a year, but on 22 February and 22 October.

9-11 November

9 November

On descending into the splendid hall, for the sand is almost to the top of the doorway, a double row of colossal figures attached to square pillars, support the roof. The placid expression of these is rather superior to those on the exterior. There are four on each side, with arms crossed and holding the scourge and crozier. Those on the right have the high conical cap & those on the left what is termed the corn measure. The walls and pillars are covered with the most interesting sculpture in excellent preservation. The roof is also in the usual style with the sacred falcon holding the two feathers. From this hall branch various apartments with a bench running round, but for what purpose has never been ascertained, the walls of these are also covered with hieroglyphics, some unfinished being only in the black outline of paint; two other apartments lead to the cella where there are four deities. They have been painted and before them is an altar cut out of the solid rock, squared at the sides, but the top is broken. This is the only thing of the kind I have seen and it is most interesting. On the sides of the wall about two feet in advance of the altar are the marks of grooves with holes for fastening of a screen probably open work or metal, to prevent the near approach of the worshippers, if they were ever admitted this far.

The smaller temple suffers in comparison with the other .... In the hall of entrance the roof is supported by square pillars ... but what with bats and an ugly kind of lizard it is most unpleasant to examine too minutely, to say nothing of more dangerous inmates. Along the surface of the sand this morning we could trace distinctly the trail of some very large serpents.

11 November

Today our friends returned from Wady Halfa. Judging from what they say of the 2nd cataract, I do not think I have lost much by staying behind. At nightfall we began to descend the stream. Thank God our vessel's prow now faces the north and civilisation. Among my crew of eight men there are two Nubians, both named Hassan, one is distinguished as Hassan Berbary, the other as Hassan Amoris, the name of his wife to whom he is very attached. He or his black friend generally accompanies me on my sketching excursions. They are most faithful and assiduous in their attention to me and, armed with my pike staff with its brass head, a beadle on a holy day is not a more important personage than is either of my trusty Nubians.

Abu Simbel was normally the most southerly point reached by travellers on the Nile. Roberts's companions appear to have sailed directly back to Cairo at this stage as they are not mentioned in the Journal again. Roberts himself slowly made his way back down the Nile, sketching more monuments until, by 9 December, he had over 100 in his portfolio. On December 11, he absentmindedly left his Nubian sketchbook on a cliff edge. Disaster was avoided when his servant returned two days later and, by great good fortune, was able to recover it.

Temples of Abu Simbel from the Nile

Here the two temples can be seen in their original picturesque setting. The Great Temple is dedicated to three gods and to a deified Ramesses II himself, and the smaller one was built in honour of Nefertari, the favourite wife of Ramesses II. It is dedicated to the goddess Hathor.

The statue to which Roberts refers as the 'young Memnon' was the representation of Ramesses II which Belzoni removed from the Ramesseum at Thebes on the instructions of Consul Salt and Burckhardt, and which was exhibited at the British Museum. The workmanship of this temple, which Roberts so admired, dates from the New Kingdom, whereas the temple at Dendera, with which Roberts compares it, was a Graeco-Roman copy of Egyptian art and was produced more than 1,000 years later. In one of the Abu Simbel lithographs, Roberts's own name has been inscribed on a statue, possibly by Haghe, the lithographer.

20-24 December

20 December

The voyage has been on the whole a very pleasant one and certainly by far the most interesting I have ever taken — my drawings I feel are not only good but of the greatest interest independant of their being mere pictures.

I am the first artist at least from England that has yet been here and there is much in this. The French work I now find conveys no idea of these splendid remains. We shall see what impression they make in England — subjects of another class of equal interest remain yet at Cairo — and equally untrodden ground.

If God spares my health I think much may be made of the splendid mosques, the tombs of the Mamelukes, & Caliphs.

21 December

Arrived safely at Cairo.

22 December

Spent all day in looking after houses and took one belonging to Osman Effendi an old Scotchman who built them & fitted them up — I am to pay 8 piastres per day or 20 pence.

24 December

Went in the afternoon and visited the Citadel; was shown some of the principal apartments, found them all modern and gaudily painted but they must look sumptuous when lighted up and filled with company — was shown the bath of Mehemet Ali, Hall of Audience etc. etc. The view from here is not excelled by any — the effect tonight was grand, the sky clouded and overcast, the setting sun burning through the haze from time to time whilst the pyramids rose black as the clouds that overhung them in the distance. The Nile reflected the glimpses of the sun whilst in some directions the city extended as far as the eye could reach, studded with minarets of the most varied and fantastic shapes, whilst that of Sultan Hassan rose in all its majesty immediately below. On the right is the passage where the unfortunate Mamelukes were butchered in cold blood only one escaping to tell the tale — but the less said of that the better, I believe they richly deserved their fate altho' we shudder at the method taken … . This is a city unequalled in the world for the picturesque and it is hitherto untrodden ground.

.. Abbas Pasha has promised me a firman, or order, to draw in the various mosques. This is all I could wish — tomorrow must be a day of exploration and then I must to work.

Cairo from the Gate of Citzenib

When the Romans conquered Egypt in 30 BC, they rebuilt the deserted fortress of Babylon and a thriving town grew up at this strategic point on the River Nile. The Arabs invaded in 641 AD and established their principal Egyptian city on the site, renaming it Fustat. In 969, the Fatimids, a North African tribe, invaded and marked out a new city slightly further north, and called it el Kahira, or Cairo.

The incursions of a Crusader king of Jerusalem in 1168 caused the Egyptians to set fire to Fustat to prevent Christian occupation. A new dynasty, the Ayyubids, was founded by Saladin, who built the great Citadel of Cairo.

This view of Cairo, from high ground to the south of the city, shows how the Citadel dominated the vista. The Sultan Hassan mosque mentioned by Roberts is on the right.

25-26 December

25 December–Christmas Day

Good morning to you in Grand Cairo some kind friends will be thinking of me as they sit down to their Christmas dinner, well God bless them all. Today I visited the tombs of the Mamelukes but I require to see them again and learn something more of them before venturing an opinion farther than that all are in the most ruinous state, some all but destroyed. In shape there is the utmost variety but in detail a sameness. Visited the mausoleum of Mehemet Ali.

26 December

Today commenced my operations in Cairo. Two large drawings of Sultan Hassan from the great square of Ramila together with the East side of this square and the mosque of the Mahmodan. This is one of the most crowded in Cairo and considering all things I was not so much annoyed as I might have expected — I made also another of the same mosque from the gate of the citadel and found assistance from the guard on duty in keeping back the crowd.

Roberts spent six weeks in Cairo, drawing some of the 400 or so mosques. He led a fairly social life with the other foreigners in the city but obviously did not regard Christmas Day as a holiday from his task. His only rest was enforced; he suffered from a stomach ailment for two days.

The house where he stayed had once belonged to a fellow Scot, known in Cairo as Osman Effendi. His real name was Donald Thomson and he had served as a drummer boy in the British army in Egypt. Captured in battle, he was offered the choice of death or adoption of the Muslim faith, and he chose the latter. He was forced to become a slave but eventually his freedom was bought by Henry Salt, the British Consul in Cairo, and by the explorer Burckhardt who employed him as an interpreter. His adventurous life ended a few years before Roberts arrived in Cairo.

Tombs of the Mamelukes

The Southern Cemetery or the Tombs of the Mamelukes contains some of the earliest Muslim tombs known in Egypt.

The old tombs provide living accommodation for homeless people — a need which existed in Roberts's day and still does today.

28 December - 1 January

28 December

I am still bewildered with the extraordinary picturesque nature of the streets and buildings of this most wonderful of all cities — the only thing more wonderful is the population, but all description of these is impossible therefore I will not even attempt it.

31 December

Last day of the year but how different from this day in London. Every day is fine, vegetables in abundance. Made one drawing today of the principal bazaar, the best drawing I have yet taken in Cairo .... I am in excellent health and in a city that surpasses all that artists can conceive. I shall not lose an hour whilst in it to cull its beauties.

1 January

Well this is the 1st day of 1839 — who knows what might take place before it ends — 'tis fortunate we do not know. I have stood in the crowded streets of Cairo jostled and stared at until I came home quite sick, no-one in looking over my sketches will ever think of the pain and trouble I have had to contend with in collecting them. Well as long as they add to the general knowledge already acquired of the various styles of architecture existing in different ages I am well satisfied.

Bazaar of the Silk Mercers

Many artists were to be attracted to the Bazaar of the Silk Mercers, with its vibrant colour and lively atmosphere. Roberts was particularly entranced by the people he saw there, and the impression of their unique appearance long remained with him.

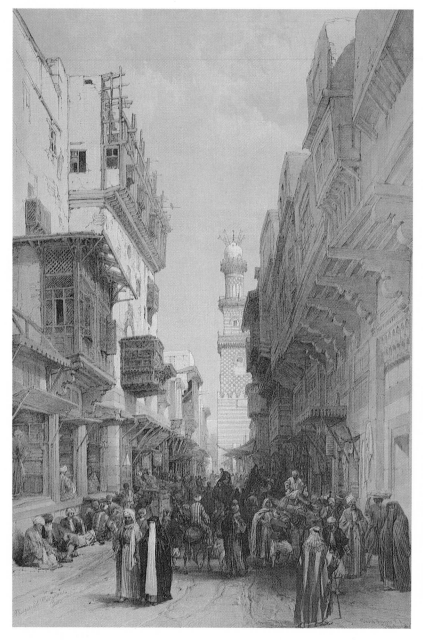

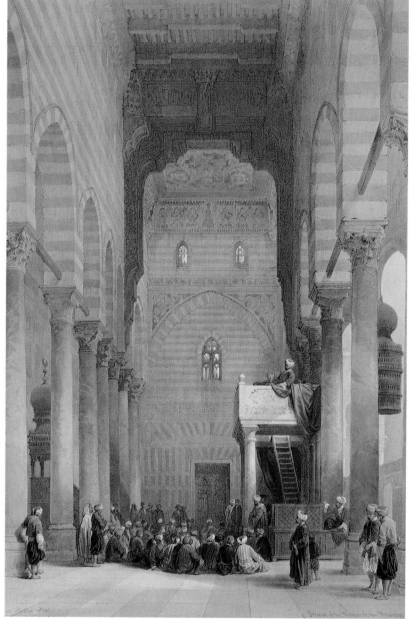

2-13 January

2 January

This morning had a visit from the consul who informed me that in order to visit the various mosques let alone make drawings, I must assume the Turkish dress. I have therefore purchased a suit today and tomorrow I must divest myself of my whiskers — this is too bad but I have taken too long a journey to stand now about trifles — I think after all I shall be the first professional man who has sat down to make a drawing — we shall see how I get on — Saturday is appointed for visiting and I have tried on my dress which fits me capitally and my servant informs me I become the dress well but he is such a thorough rogue, I can believe him in nothing. What would my friends in England say to see me masquerading in this uniform but after all my object can be accomplished in no other way, no Christian being allowed to enter these places at all. My object is to get at these remains of a bygone age, all now fast hastening to decay, many already in total ruin. The day was, and not long since, that a Christian life would have been forfeited for visiting them. Today being far from well I took a stroll through a part of the city I had not hitherto visited and was more and more surprised at the splendour of its remains — all the artists in Europe could hardly hunt up its picturesque remains in six months.

Roberts's plans for his trip to Syria involved trying to hire camels but there was a shortage of these desert animals because of the imminent departure of a pilgrimage to Mecca. He decided to ride out to watch the dramatic departure of the caravan.

13 January

Today being the one appointed for the grand caravan setting out for Mecca, this being the first of the new moon … . It was certainly a most extraordinary gathering of all tribes and of all nations, but it was not quite so numerous as I had expected; probably the number of camels did not exceed two thousand with about two or three hundred horse … . From where we sat the scene was most striking. All went to midday prayers, the heads of all the camels faced the east together with those of the worshippers. On a signal being given the piece of ordnance was discharged and the whole mass began to move.

Far left: Mosque of el Mooristan

Left: Interior of the Mosque of the Metwalis

No longer confined to drawing the exterior of the mosques since he had acquired a Turkish disguise and two bodyguards, Roberts revelled in the opportunity to enter the precincts and sketch in peace.

The Holy Land

Roberts spent much of January completing his portfolio of drawings of Cairo and finalising the arrangements for his journey to the Holy Land.

Two entries for his diary in January record his fear that he might not be able to visit Jerusalem because of an outbreak of plague, and his conviction that the difficulties and dangers to be endured would be compensated for by the unique opportunities for sketching little-known sights.

21 January

Spent all day in packing and arranging my sketches. Afterwards I waited on the consul when to my utter dismay he informed me in a casual conversation that the plague had been in Jerusalem for the last three months and was on the increase! That a cordon was drawn around and that independent of the chance of contagion in visiting the city a quarantine must take place! This is most perplexing and after I have everything ready too! To think of visiting Syria without seeing Jerusalem would be as bad as going to England and not seeing London, indeed it would be worse as the home of most that is important in scriptural history is laid in the capital. It is most provoking if I must give it up — I know not what to do.

29 January

This morning having at last made up my mind I have settled on proceeding to Syria by the way of Mount Sinai and Petra to Hebron and Jerusalem. It will be a long and fatiguing journey to say nothing of the expense ... I don't know how I shall get on. I am in excellent health and care nothing for fatigue or, as far as I am concerned, for dangers but there are those at home who do — well I have no doubt all will end well. Then for home with one of the richest folios that ever left the East. It is worth the hazard.

Roberts's entry for 6 February describes his travelling companions for the expedition.

6 February

Having made arrangements with my friend Mr Pell to effect the journey together — each having his own tents, servants — an agreement was entered into with the Sheik of the tribe of the Beni Said to find camels to convey us together with our baggage and servants to the Convent of Saint Catherine on Mount Sinai and from thence to Akaba. The sum agreed was as follows: 250 piastres for each camel to Akaba, or about £2.10.0d. My friend Mr Pell taking with him a young Egyptian, Ishmael Effendi in the service of Mehemet Ali, educated in England and speaks English fluently, an Abyssinian boy called Farrag and an Arab servant. Mr John Kinnear who, having some spare time and a great desire to visit Petra, proposed joining us and sharing my tent, his servant together with mine making a strong party — being eight in all and well-armed — taking twenty-one camels to carry provisions for the journey. All today occupied in buying provisions for our journey through the desert — waited on Colonel Campbell and thanked him for all his kindness to me during my stay in this country — he promises me letters to Jerusalem, Damascus and Beirout ...

Roberts's journey in the Holy Land.

Although all of the territories covered in Roberts's journey were under the control of Mehemet Ali in 1839, the area is currently divided between Egypt, Jordan, Israel and Lebanon.

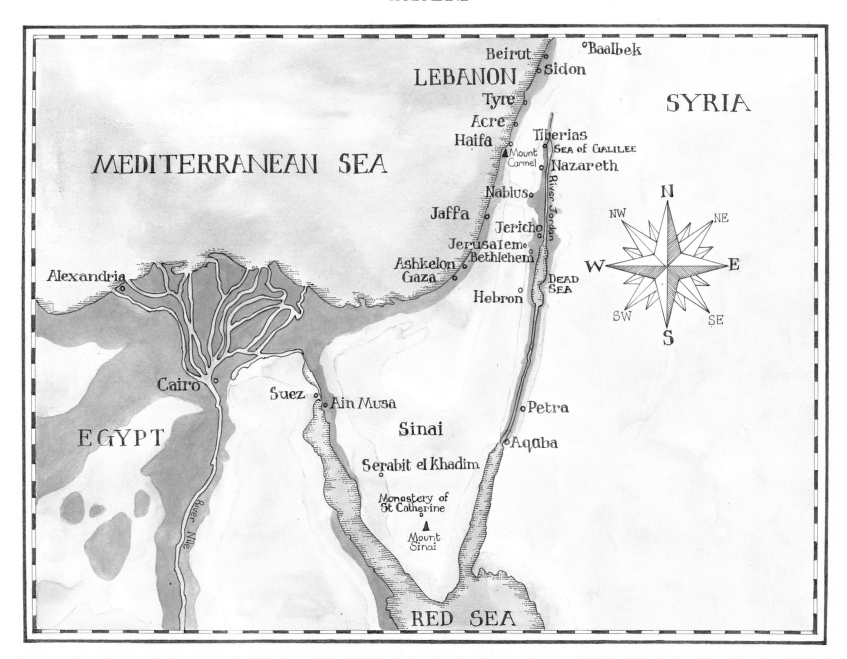

6-10 *February*

6 February

Was introduced yesterday to the celebrated Sheik of the Bedowins and his followers — they appear a wild family, but I am much pleased with their countenances, and am very much mistaken if they turn out otherwise than trustworthy. Altogether things look far better than they did and I begin to think I shall enjoy the journey.

7 February

In the afternoon left Cairo and encamped in the desert — for my first night in a tent. It passed off pretty well.

10 February

Came in sight of Suez, and the Red Sea, country around a perfect desert not a shrub or tree to be met with, the whole line of the route marked only by the mouldering skeletons of camels, from the great traffic, now reopened betwixt Cairo & the Red Sea. Suez ... this is a wretched place. During the night the steamer from Bombay arrived and all was bustle. The bazaars are of a piece with the rest of the town but what a painter would call picturesque. Our route lay round the upper part of the Gulf — and through a swamp or marsh, still the clouds of sand were so overwhelming that about midday we were obliged to pull up, our tents were pitched close to the sea — night wet and cold — but slept soundly.

In a letter to his only daughter, Christine, Roberts described his preparations for the journey:
> I have provided everything requisite for my journey. A tent (a very gay one, I assure you), skins for carrying water, pewter dishes, provisions of all sorts, not forgetting a brace of Turkish pistols, and a warm covering for the night. Imagine me mounted on my camel, my black servant on another, and two men with my tent and luggage; the other two gentlemen similarly furnished and accoutred, surrounded by a host of the children of the desert.

In Kinnear's account of this journey he envies the artist's warm covering:
I cannot say that I have slept very comfortably this first night in our tent, it was bitterly cold, and I began to envy my friend Roberts a little the comfortable mattress, blankets, sheets and pillows with which he had provided himself.

Above: Arabs of the Desert

Right: Suez

The town of Suez was founded in the 15th century but it was not until it became a port for sailings to India that it assumed any major importance.

11-12 February

11 February

Rather a row with our Arabs, found out that the entire quantity of corn that the camels had been loaded with, instead of being for their feed during the journey, was principally seed corn, for their forthcoming harvest — their having lost their last year's corn in toto, from drought.

12 February

Woke with fresh spirits morning delightful wind changed to the east — walked for two hours, and then spreading our carpets partook of our frugal breakfast. On my right is the sea, with a high range of bold and picturesque mountains, with headlands stretching far to the south, near their base lies the small, and at this distance, pretty town of Suez, and reflected in the blue waters in the blaze of the burning sun — a few fishing craft leave to give animation to a scene that would otherwise be lifeless … . In two hours we reached the Wells of Moses. They are 15 in all, surrounded by a few stunted palm trees, here we had our repast.

Kinnear recalls in his journal:
After leaving our encampment this morning we again came in sight of the sea and about nine o'clock arrived at Ayn Mousa 'the fountains of Moses' where the Israelites are supposed to have landed on coming up out of the Red Sea. A few wild palm trees, shaggy and unpruned, grow beside the wells, and form, I think, a more picturesque feature in the landscape than the date palms of Egypt with their long bare stems and tufted heads; though these too are very beautiful. The water has a brackish taste: but we were fain to replenish our skins with it, as our Nile water was expended, and we had found that of Suez quite undrinkable.

Ain Mousa

According to tradition, these are the springs which Moses caused miraculously to appear for the Israelites after they had safely crossed the Red Sea. Today, the visitor may cross the Suez Canal to reach the site by means of a tunnel but once there, little will have changed since the days of Roberts's visit.

15-16 February

15 February

We are now in the midst of the wilderness of Sinai ... we have now been nine days traversing this waste, and with the exception of meeting one or two Arabs of the same tribe, on the way to Egypt to buy corn — we seem as if cut off from the world. The fifth and sixth day of our route lay by the shores of the Red Sea ... the hills today on each side of us are a soft sandstone and are more grand and picturesque in their forms. I am every day more delighted with the manly intelligent countenance of our Bedowins — our friend Ishmael is of the greatest service to us in translating or rather interpreting to us, the account they give us of their tribe, their laws, customs etc. Their country is in the immediate neighbourhood of Sinai — and they are paid for the protection or guardianship of the Convent of Saint Catherine. Their tribe consists of about one hundred men ... 300 camels, besides goats & sheep — a great part of the latter was last year lost, as well as their crops from the excessive drought.

16 February

Starting at 7 we travelled on foot for an hour and a half; arrived at the foot of the mountains we took our frugal repast previous to ascending, and leaving our camels followed our guide Beshara. Our course lay in the bed of a mountain torrent ... . Having attained the boundary of the ravine we began to clamber up the steep sides of the mountain, our road, if such it could be called, was only to be traced by a few stones piled one above another at certain distances some parts of it lay along the brink of a precipice where one false step would have been fatal, and at other times we had to clamber up the face of the rock with greatest difficulty; at last we attained the summit and to my surprise, instead of the few stones I had expected to see I found an Egyptian temple.

Kinnear gives a description of the ruins: The ruins appear from a little distance a group of upright stones amidst a confused mass of fallen masonry, and bear a considerable resemblance to an old churchyard. The upright tablets are from six to eight feet in height, and about two feet broad, and are arched at the top. They are covered on both sides with hieroglyphics; but on the side exposed to the northern blasts, the inscriptions are nearly obliterated ... . We rode through a narrow defile, terminating in a steep mound of stones and mountain wrack, where we were obliged to dismount and ascend on foot driving the dromedaries before us ... . The country became more gloomy as we proceeded.

The mountains had a scorched, metallic appearance, and the valleys were so encumbered with masses of rock and sharp stones, that our progress was slow and painful. At sunset we entered a fine open valley ... . It was nearly dark when we perceived a fire at the upper end of the valley; and dismounting from my dromedary, I walked on and found our tents pitched, and dinner — such as it was — in preparation.

Gebel Garaba

These ruins at Sarabit el-Khadim were correctly identified by Roberts and Kinnear as a temple, although earlier visitors had supposed them to be the remains of a cemetery. The temple was dedicated to Hathor, known by her local worshippers as 'the Mistress of the Turquoise'.

18 February

We started at twelve for the convent of Saint Catherine and after winding through a terrific pass for about three hours night closed around us before we could reach the convent; the effect of the setting sun gilding the high peaks of the pass, whilst the ravine itself was a mass of shadow, far surpassed everything of the kind I have ever witnessed. We reached the convent about seven o'clock and after some little delay, a small twinkling light appeared at a great height in the wall, and on looking up a black bearded monk could just be distinguished reconnoitering our party, this lasted only a few seconds, and after some time during which he was probably announcing our arrival to the superior, another door, covered with plates of iron, was unbolted and a trap raised. A light was first lowered by a rope, and afterwards some faggots were thrown down for the Arabs to make a fire, on the kindling of which the rope by which we were to be drawn up was lowered. At this time nothing could exceed the picturesque effect of the weary Arabs and camels round the newly lighted fire. We were drawn up one by one our elbows and knees receiving sundry thumps and bumps in the course of the ascent. We were ushered through a labyrinth of passages and staircases to the dormitories we were to occupy for the night. The superior received us in person with the greatest attention and kindness. A supper was soon provided of rice and dried dates and never did poor pilgrim sleep more soundly than I under the hospitable roof of the monks of St Catherine.

Approach to Mount Sinai

Saint Catherine's monastery, built by the Emperor Justinian in the sixth century, is said to be the oldest continuously inhabited building in the world. Traditionally revered as housing the site of the Burning Bush of Moses, it nestles at the feet of two mountains; one, Gebel Musa, referred to by Roberts as Mount Sinai, is believed to be the mountain ascended by Moses to receive the Ten Commandments.

The second and higher peak, Gebel Katerin, referred to by Roberts as Mount Horeb, is where Saint Catherine's body is said to have been deposited by angels after her martyrdom under the Emperor Maxentius (306-312). Five centuries later, her remains were removed by monks to a tomb within the monastery.

The monks survived Muslim occupation of the area partly due to the monastery's claim to hold a charter of protection given by the Prophet himself, but also because a mosque was built within its walls. Archaeological work indicates that in the 11th century, the mosque was hurriedly converted from a sixth century guest house — perhaps because the monks were given advance warning of an invading Muslim army. Despite severe damage in the earthquake of 1312, much of the wall surrounding the monastery dates back to the sixth century. For security reasons, the original gate was walled up and the only access for many years was by winch. The French expedition of 1801 restored much of the wall and made a new gate.

19 February

The convent is a large square enclosure, the walls with flanking towers are built of hewn granite.

The only entrance is by an opening in the wall at the height of 30 feet and this strongly guarded by an iron door; a rope is lowered and raised by a capstan. Inside the walls it appears a small town for besides various apartments and store houses for the monks, it contained a chapel and a mosque with its minaret, the former said to be built on the site of the burning bush and the latter by the Prophet Mahomet. The monks claim that during his stay on the summit of Sinai he was received at the convent with the greatest respect; having preached a sermon he informed the monks that with their permission he would erect a mosque on the spot and give them a written document for their protection against his followers. A copy of this is still shown, the original is said to be at Constantinopole ... there stands the mosque, its minaret surmounted by the crescent and whenever a Moslem of any consequence visits the mount, for it is held in equal veneration by the Mahomedans and Christians, they perform their ablutions here and go through their form of worship.

The brotherhood wear a small black cap with a striped woollen abba or cloak of the brown and white wool of the goats of the mountain.

It is impossible to come to the truth as to the number of the monks but I do not think they exceed seventeen if indeed there are as many. No Arabs are admitted within the walls except one or two as servants.

Left: Convent of Saint Catherine

with Mount Horeb

This region was first visited by pilgrims at the end of the 4th century AD when the Roman Lady Etheria claimed to have found the Burning Bush and a church on the site.

Right: Principal Court of the Convent

of Saint Catherine

The interior of the monastery has changed little over the centuries. A corrugated iron roof to the church, a bell tower erected in 1871 and a 20th century guest wing are the alterations made since Roberts's visit.

Above: Ascent to the Summit of Mount Sinai

Early pilgrims were required to ascend the 3,000 steps to the summit, sometimes on their knees, before being absolved of their sins.

Right: Encampment of the Oulad Said

20-25 February

20 February

Today we ascended to the summit of Sinai which took us two hours. Near the top are two small chapels, one covers the cave where Elijah was fed by the ravens and the other is dedicated to Elias and on the summit are two others; one where Moses received the tables of the law and the other belongs to the Mahomedans; immediately under it is pointed out the footmark of the camel which carried him from Mount Ararat to Mecca. The view from the top is the most sublime that can be imagined.

22 February

Went to the summit of Mount Horeb and descended into the valley on the west. Made a drawing of the rock of Moses said to be the same from which the waters gushed forth to the thirsty multitude. Today we took leave of our kind friends the monks of St Catherine; it would be impossible to speak too highly of the attention and kindness with which we have been treated during our stay particularly by the superior. Our baggage was forwarded early in the morning and in the afternoon we found our caravan encamped in a beautiful Wady amidst the mountains. After a pleasant gossip we retired.

24 February

Leaving the granite mountains of Sinai our course now winds amongst high rocks of sandstone with a level bed of sand interspersed with bushes principally of the wild thyme which the camels are very fond of; the fragrance from it is delicious and almost the only scent to be found in the desert.

25 February

After two hours walk through a wild and picturesque ravine we descended upon the Red Sea or Gulf of Akaba yesterday. The sirocco or south wind set in today. It blew a hurricane with dense clouds of sand, so that we could scarcely see six yards before us; our guide Beshara fairly lost his way and the storm of sand was so dense that we were on the edge of the sea for some time without knowing it, however after an hour or two's groping we came up to the caravan and our servants pitched the tents.

26-27 February

26 February

This morning delightful, all appearance of the sirocco disappeared and the wind changed to the eastward. One of the Arab fishermen who had followed our caravan threw in his net and filled his wallet with a beautiful pair of fish similar to salmon, which we enjoyed amazingly at our breakfast. I bathed before breakfast in the Red Sea and found it truly refreshing, the heat was excessive & I would have given anything for a draught of fresh water, our own having become wretched and perfectly undrinkable. Our road lay nearly all day along the sea shore but towards evening we turned up into the hills to avoid some headland that runs into the sea.

27 February

Near where we encamped for the night and close by a shoulder of the chain of mountains that juts into the sea, is a small island called the Isle of Graia covered with the ruins of an ancient fortress. We could learn nothing of its history from the Sheik of the Beni Said but a foolish story of it having commanded the Gulph and that a chain was drawn across from the opposite side which is six miles distant. Having bathed again we resumed our ride round the Gulph which would have been delightful could we have forgotten our hunger and thirst, for through mismanagement the last drops of our wretched water were exhausted and this morning we were without any. Our caravan hurried on to the fortress of Akaba where we arrived about 12 o'clock. Our camels and Arab attendants made a very formidable appearance before the pygmy fortress and the Governor and Commandant, its garrison and all about it were in active motion to receive us. The fortress was offered for our accommodation but was declined, we having fixed upon a spot immediately above it for our encampment, these worthy authorities however strongly objected to it, saying that they would not be answerable for our safety unless we pitched our tents between the fort and the sea, which we had eventually to do.

Isle of Graia

It is now thought that this island of Jezirat el Fara'un may possibly have been the biblical port of Ezion Geber, constructed for King Solomon by the Phoenicians.

1-2 March

1 March

Our Arabs took their departure for the neighbourhood of Sinai, excepting the Sheik Hussein and our faithful Beshara. We have as yet heard nothing of the Alloweens. Heartily tired of this wretched place every article is double and triple the price of what we pay at Cairo; with the exception of a few dates nothing is raised in its neighbourhood, every article for its consumption being brought from Cairo and sold to the Arabs by them evidently at any price they think proper to ask. The fortress itself is kept up solely for the protection of the Hadjj or Caravan to Mecca from Cairo.

Fortress of Aqaba

Upon being received by the governor in the fortress of Aqaba, Roberts and his group discovered that letters of introduction to the governor and Sheik of the Alloween, which had been promised in Cairo, had not arrived. The Sheik then had to be sent for, which involved a delay of several days and much frustration to the party.

2 March

This morning the Sheik of the Alloween arrived and a grand palavar ensued. The tent was filled, the divan being arranged in all the state of the East .... Coffee having been twice served a general conversation took place as to the route to Hebron, the way we had fixed on being objected to as one tribe there was at war with the Government. As we found it impossible to come to terms we ordered breakfast and the assembly broke up .... We opened the conference as to terms and upon much pressing, the Sheik of the Alloween named a sum which was seven thousand five hundred piastres. This was so far beyond what we had expected that we were perfectly amazed .... We had given up all hope of coming to an agreement ... when Hussein of the Beni Said took him aside and after a great deal of spluttering they again entered our tent and fresh proposals were made, all of which were rejected .... It was then proposed that in order to put an end to their haggling, which has already consumed much time, we should make an addition of 500 to the 4,000 we had already proposed; seeing that we were determined, after some time this was agreed to, coffee was again served and the agreement drawn up by Ishmael in which the Sheik guaranteed our safe passage to Hebron by the way of Wady Moosa or Petra, staying at the latter place as long as we thought proper, for 4,500 piastres .... Thus was our bargain finished which consumed more time in settling than all the bargains I ever made put together and in which diplomacy was carried as far on both sides as if kingdoms had depended on it .... After all can Petra be worth all the risk, expense and delay it has cost us?

Kinnear: Akaba is a mere group of wretched hovels, and it is difficult to conjecture how the people contrive to live. Where Solomon had his navy of ships, there is not a single boat to be found; and a solitary fisherman may be seen, on a calm day, paddling himself out to sea astride the trunk of a palm tree. The fortress ... is garrisoned by a small number of irregular troops, who appear to have nothing to do but to waste the Pasha's powder in shooting all day at a mark .... The weather was so oppressively hot that we moved very little out, except in the afternoon to bathe; and we were never allowed for any length of time, to enjoy the privacy of our own tent without interruption.

6 March

Petra. We encamped in the centre of this extraordinary city or rather the remains of it. Situated in the midst of mountains and though surrounded by the desert, abounding in every vegetable production. The difficulty of access to it is so great that the curse seems still to hang over it. The Sheik insisted on our leaving our tents at the foot of the mountains … but we were determined to take all our baggage and accordingly began to ascend the ravine, the Sheik looking unutterable things and swearing we should be the last travellers he would ever conduct to Wady Moosa. Our path was still in the base of the stream but after about an hour's march we began to ascend the mountains by a rugged and tangled mountain track; leaving our baggage we continued to ascend till we attained a great height … . We were on the point of descending into the valley of Petra when we were surrounded by a body of Arabs who told us by gestures that were not mistaken, that all further progress was debarred us; fortunately Ishmael was with us and a parley ensued in which the Sheik of the Wady informed us that the Sheik of the Alloweens had no right to enter the valley. A long statement of their grievances was entered into and finding we were not likely to be admitted into the city, breakfast was spread and we invited the Sheik of Wady Moosa to partake of it with us till the Sheik of

the Alloween and the camels arrived … . The caravan at last appeared but quite a different scene took place to what we expected, instead of fighting they embraced each other kissing on both cheeks. The Sheik of the Alloweens ordered each to mount his camel and we descended into the valley and pitched our tents in the very centre of the city.

John Kinnear recorded:
We entered the valley from the south at a point from which a view of nearly the whole of it burst at once upon our sight. My expectations were far more than realized. Much as I had heard of the wonderful excavations of Petra, I had formed a very inadequate idea of their state of preservation, of the number of sculptured façades, porticos, and fanciful designs which surround the valley, or of the extent of the valley itself. It is certainly one of the most wonderful scenes in the world. The eye wanders in amazement from the stupendous rampart of rocks which surrounds the valley to the porticos and ornamental doorways sculptured on its surface. The dark yawning entrances of the temples and tombs, and the long ranges of excavated chambers, give an air of emptiness and desolation to the scene.

Site of Petra South

In Biblical times, this was the land of Edom but by the fourth century BC Nabatean kings were presiding over a flourishing trading nation. Petra was at the point of convergence of several principal caravan routes and the Nabatean success in storing water contributed to the prosperity of the area.

The Romans made several attempts to conquer the kingdom and finally succeeded in 106 AD. The Roman influence on the architecture was considerable but slowly the city began to decline until, by the time of the Arab conquest in the seventh century, it was of no importance and only partially occupied.

The Crusaders built a fort there but Petra then became a hidden city to European eyes, until it was discovered by Jean Louis Burckhardt in 1812.

6 March

After smoking and taking a cup of coffee we attempted to reach the ruins by force, but were as forcibly driven back, although most of us were armed with clubs and matchlock guns; they were determined and we were anxious to avoid coming to an open rupture with them. What they stated appeared reasonable enough: that the Sheik of the Alloween got all the money for showing a place which he had no right to enter, and that they ought to have at least a share of it; a great dispute took place between them which lasted for some time, till we sent for them to our tents and offered to make any reasonable accommodation. The sum asked for was so exorbitant that we would not agree to it, particularly as no traveller had ever had to pay tribute here before, still it was most provoking to be in the midst of the city and not allowed to approach a single object. I had previously in my anxiety to see the first temple in the valley, been detained, a sort of prisoner, for half an hour, during the pitching of the tents. We told them we had come quite unprepared for any demands of this kind and with barely sufficient to take us to Hebron, still we would satisfy them as far as it was in our power if they would guarantee our safety during our stay in Petra; we therefore agreed to give him 100 piastres each, he having previously come down to 500 … . He at last agreed to take 300 and

this unpleasant affair was amicably settled; coffee was ordered, a goat killed for the Arabs and another for ourselves, and all invited to dine with us every day during our stay.

Our first stroll was to the Khasne and I am at a loss whether to say I was most surprised by the building itself or the extraordinary nature of its position. … the whole is far beyond any idea I had ever formed of it, both in magnitude and situation. The whole valley is strewn with ruins, the style of the architecture varied in its leading features

from most others of the same nature I have previously seen and in its parts is a curious combination of the Egyptian and the Roman and Greek order.

Kinnear: The Khasne owes much of its effect to the suddenness with which it bursts on the sight, and the strange contrast which its fanciful design, and the freshness of its colour, form with the rugged and weather-stained crags by which it is surrounded. Standing, as it were, in an immense niche in the face of the rock, the whole edifice has been wonderfully preserved from the effects of the weather; while the fine colour of the stone, which is a beautiful pink, and the perfect preservation of the most minute details, and delicate carving give it all the appearance of having been recently finished.

Far left: Excavations at the Eastern end of Petra

Above: El Khasne

El Khasne means the treasury, and the decorative urn on top of the façade was believed to hold the treasure of a magician pharaoh; the surface bears witness to local attempts to shatter it with bullets and release the booty. Scholars now believe that this, the best preserved monument in Petra, was built as a temple. It has a wonderfully dramatic and solitary position opposite the entrance of the Siq.

7-8 March

7 March

This morning a muster of the whole armed tribe took place and much business was transacted in their way. Three Sheiks presided and each spoke by turns; after two hours consultation they dispersed without further annoyance to us. All is now tolerably quiet and by feeding the Arabs with a sheep a day we remain unmolested.

I am more and more bewildered with the extent of this extraordinary city; not only the city which must be two miles in extent by nearly the same in breadth, but every ravine has been inhabited even to the tops of the mountains. The valley itself has been filled with temples, public buildings, triumphal arches and bridges all of which are laid prostrate with the exception of one triumphal arch and one temple and the portico of this has fallen.

8 March

Today, accompanied by a guard of Arabs we wound our way up a steep ravine, a broken staircase extending to the whole length which was nearly a mile, we at length reached the object of our journey which was a building, rarely visited, called El Deir or the Convent. It is hewn out of the face of the rock, and is of greater magnitude than the Khasne being upward of one hundred feet in height and one thousand feet above the level of the city.

Far left: Meeting of Arabs

Left: El Deir

Like the Khasne, this building was originally a temple but crosses carved on the wall suggest it was later used for Christian worship, hence its Arabic name meaning 'the monastery'.

9-10 March

9 March

Mr P- and I this morning explored the grand entrance to Petra. It may be about a mile in length, winding between the high rocks by which the valley is enclosed, in many parts they overhang, so as to meet within a foot of each other but in others are perpendicular and ranging from three to six hundred feet in height. Man, in this vast chasm dwindles into nothing, yet this was the grand entrance into Petra and is still used by the Arabs in spite of the torrents which rush through it, a large caravan of about 40 camels belonging to Gaza passed through it yesterday … . Between the main entrance and the meadow land is the necropolis; some of the tombs hewn out of solid rock so as to form isolated temples, are still in spite of their mutilated condition of the most magnificent kind; many are formed out of the rock itself and represent porticos with colonnades on each side; one I observed with the doric columns of the most pure Greek taste; they appear now to be used as pens for cattle.

10 March

Today all seemed amicably settled with the Sheik of Wady Moosa a petition has been drawn up, to the authorities in Cairo requesting his appointment to guard all travellers for the future, he, the Sheik guaranteeing their safety against the hostile Arabs. Mr P- has undertaken to present it at Cairo.

The rain set in but notwithstanding, I have made several sketches of the leading features of this extraordinary place.

Left: The Arch across the Ravine

Only the remains of the arch across the ravine can now be seen although it was still standing at the end of the 19th century. The channels cut in the rock carried water.

Right: The Necropolis, Petra

The so-called 'Obelisk' tomb is situated outside the Siq and is the only monument at Petra to show clear evidence of Egyptian influence. It is believed to have been constructed around 250 BC either for, or by, someone acquainted with Ptolemaic Egypt. The monolithic blocks in the foreground are known as the 'Djin' blocks and their exact purpose is unknown, although they are thought to be tombs.

11 March

Though now lulled by the terror in which the name of Mehemet Ali is held, the desert is still the desert and Edom as perilous to travellers … .

The attack made upon us and the contribution levied showed that they had still the will as well as the power to practise their old profession; were it not that we were under the guardianship of the sheik of one of the most powerful tribes of the desert, I have no doubt, that instead of their demands being limited to contribution in money we should have been stripped of all we had, as Burckhardt himself was. Notwithstanding all this I have roamed this vast city sketch book in hand, perfectly alone and I may say have met with very little molestation. The Arabs themselves here warned us to keep a sharp lookout as the Wady has a bad name but it is better than it used to be. Two days ago they stole a metal soup tureen which they probably supposed to be silver. The Sheik said he knew the thief and left us to go in search of him promising to return with it or meet us at the foot of the mountains, but we have not yet seen him.

After a wet day, we lay down in our tents which were damp, cold and comfortless … tired and wet we went to our mats and notwithstanding the heavy patter of the rain were soon asleep. In the middle of the night I was roused by the cry of robbers. All was confusion, the Sheik shouting to each of his tribe by name. P- exclaiming that they had carried off his double-barrelled pistols and a bag of shot, and calling for mine. Five of them slept in the tent together, P- and an Abyssinian boy his servant, the two Sheiks and Ismael Effendi. On account of the rain the Arabs had gone for shelter to one of the numerous caves above. They slept with a light in the tent and in groping about the thieves upset some books which awoke P- who sleeping with his clothes on, was on his feet in an instant; as he rose he saw the canvas of the side of the tent fall, but they had got the start of him and a brace of English pistols, a bag with percussion caps, and a box containing wax candles had disappeared. Our guard took up their station when too late, but we were still uncertain whether a general attack might now be intended.

The night however passed quietly enough and at eight next morning the camels were loaded and our caravan in motion. I repeatedly turned to look back upon this doomed city, so sad a memorial of Divine judgement, in its strength it must have scorned all human means of destruction, placed as it is in the very bosom of impenetrable mountains, its walls so strongly formed by nature that compared to them the works of man shrink into insignificance.

Kinnear: One gets wonderfully accustomed to such adventures in this country; and, although in the narration it may appear sufficiently exciting to disturb one's rest, we slept very soundly, after arranging our tent in such a manner that no one could enter without awaking us. We left the valley of Petra nearly at the same point at which we had entered it, leaving to the left the ruins of a temple, of which a single column remains standing. The grey mists were rolling rapidly upwards, over the bare and rugged sides of the mountain; but the clouds gradually broke up, disclosing larger and larger portions of blue sky; and the rain storm, with which we had been threatened the evening before, passed away with only a gentle shower. We talked of ascending to Aaron's tomb, a modern building, which crowns the highest peak; but Hussein urged us to proceed without delay; and, after the example we had had of the treachery of the Fellaheen, we thought it might be more prudent to listen for once to his advice, and not to stop till we had placed the mountains between us and Wady Mousa.

The Theatre

This was a Roman construction and building it involved hacking away the façades of a whole street of tombs, Kinnear's 'sort of corridor'.

Kinnear: It is an immense semi-circular excavation, containing thirty-three rows of benches, and capable of accommodating between three and four thousand persons. It is in a wonderful state of preservation, the benches and the steps leading from the lower to the upper tiers being nearly entire. Above the highest tier, there is a sort of corridor in which there are several doors leading to small excavated chambers. Above this the rock rises to a sufficient height to have shaded the whole audience from the sun. There are no remains of the stage, which was probably built, but the bases of the columns in the proscenium still remain in their original places, hidden amongst the grass and wild flowers.

12-17 March

12 March

Kinnear: About mid-day we came to a small encampment of Bedaweens; and observing that they had a flock of goats and a few sheep, we rode towards the tents; for our larder was empty, and so fair an opportunity of replenishing it was not to be missed. While we were bargaining for a sheep, two women came to offer us milk. They had large rings in their noses, and, had they worn the veil, they might have passed for beauties, for their eyes were very fine, but their faces far from agreeable. The men were very civil, and did not ask more than three times the price which we paid them for the sheep. About four o'clock, we came to a few bare, leafless, stag-horn looking trees, where Sheik Hussein proposed to halt, as it was the only place within many hours where firewood was to be found. ... none of us felt inclined to ride further. I believe most of the party were impatient for the death of the unlucky sheep, which had been trotting along with us for the last three or four hours, unconscious of its approaching fate.

16 March

On turning the side of a hill the little town of Hebron bursts upon us. Its situation is beautiful and the houses glittered in the noonday sun and after the wretched hovels of Egypt appeared to have a look of almost English cleanliness. The children who came out as we approached I fancied were the most beautiful I had ever seen ... I learnt here that the plague rages at Jerusalem and in the event of escaping it 18 days quarantine in the cave of Elisha. Having pitched our tents in the burial ground of the new town we waited upon the Governor and showed our passports.

17 March

I made two coloured sketches of the town and endeavoured to procure an entrance to the mosque containing the tomb of Abraham, Jacob, Joseph and Rebecca, but I found it was quite impossible .... I was told by the Governor that the town contains thirteen hundred families, four Jewish and one Christian; from the Christian family we received the most marked attention. They invited us to pass the night at their house which we did.

Kinnear: We did not find the interior of the town to correspond with its external beauty. The streets are steep, dark, and very dirty, and the bazaars neither extensive nor well stocked. We found that it would be useless, if not dangerous, to enter their mosque. I have no doubt that the plague had reached Hebron, although it had not been officially noticed, nor any quarantine established. There had been four or five deaths the day before we arrived; on the 17th there were six; and this day (the 18th) seven funerals. The 'mourning women' were heard continually in the streets; and groups of females, enveloped in their long white veils, were all day seated among the tombs, screaming and slapping their faces, or sitting in mournful silence by the new graves.

Hebron

According to religious tradition, Abraham and his followers lived in Hebron and when his wife Sarah died, he buried her in a cave he bought from Ephron the Hittite. Abraham and several of his descendants were buried in the same tomb, Machpelah, and King Herod constructed a building over it. In Byzantine times, it became a church and the Muslims in the seventh century converted it into a mosque. The Crusaders took Hebron and held it briefly, and the mosque became a church again. After the capture of the town by the Muslims in 1267, the building was again converted to a mosque, which it has remained.

18-23 March

18 March

Kinnear: Late in the afternoon we started on foot, and rode a little way on the camels; but notwithstanding our dromedary riding for a month before, I found the twisting motion of the camel so intolerable, that, although we only travelled four hours, it was one of the most uncomfortable journeys I ever made. Anyone who is in the habit of riding on horseback will find no great fatigue or inconvenience in riding a dromedary, though his very long step is at first a little unpleasant; but the camel has a heavy, jolting gait, and as he moves both feet on each side together, your back is twisted at every step, and your head is kept nodding like a Chinese joss.

20 March

Continuing to pass through a richly cultivated country we approached Gaza through extensive olive groves, the trees of great antiquity but apparently much neglected. We reached Gaza about 12. It is situated on a height and surrounded by gardens and when fortified and in its glory must have been a noble place. It stands about two miles from the sea and is sheltered from it by high hills of sand so that to all appearances it is an inland town. None of its former grandeur

remains; the inhabitants appear wretchedly poor and there are not even the ruins of any buildings of consequence left. The town and mosques appear to be built of the remains of its former buildings; every house has fragments of marble sculpture and columns and on passing through a wretched suburb today, I noticed that one of the houses had its roof propped up in the centre by a number of beautifully sculptured capitals piled one above another.

23 March

Camels were promised to us yesterday and again today but we are disappointed — 400 troops being about to leave, all that can be had are seized by the Governor. It is most annoying to be obliged to lose so much time .... The Governor only procured us 5 camels instead of nine, but rather than stay we started for Jaffa with these for our baggage. Walking even in Turkish slippers is better than staying here.

Kinnear: Of the Gaza of the Philistines there is no vestige remaining; and it was probably not on the site of the present town, although Baumgarten and some of the early travellers assert that they saw the remains of the temple of Dagon here.

Gaza

Samson was brought to Gaza after he was ensnared by Delilah and blinded. He was put to grinding corn and after his hair had grown again, it was Gaza's temple of Dagon that he demolished. Of the five major Philistine cities, Askelon, Asdod and Gaza were on the coast and Ekron and Gath were inland — these two remain unidentified by archaeologists. A mound in the north east quarter of modern Gaza is all that remains, and it has revealed very little of the ancient town.

24 March

Starting very early we unfortunately passed Askelon hours before we were aware of it. Mr P- and I immediately returned. It is close upon the sea … . It has been surrounded by high ramparts which occupy the line of hills encompassing the ancient city, but they are now in ruins. The ground within slopes towards the sea; its mole or harbour has long ago been swept away and probably this led to the desertion of the city. Many ancient granite pillars used in its construction still exist but most of these are broken. The ruins of the ancient city may be about 2 miles in circuit. Ibrim Pasha has caused a great part to be excavated for the purpose of getting the stone and marble to construct a modern city. The most interesting remains here have been laid open; one temple with its pillars of grey granite entire in one piece but prostrate … . In the foundations of one of the buildings lay a very large female statue in white marble. The bases of the columns with the walls and pavement of an early Christian church has been laid open … . The village is quite modern and the whole place strewed with granite and marble columns.

Kinnear: To the westward of the road to Jaffa, within a short distance of the sea, are the ruins of Askelon. After leaving the culti-vated country, and passing among some low sand-hills, you come to a long line of broken

wall, part of the defences, probably, erected during the Crusades, when the strength of its position caused the possession of Askelon to be often warmly contested. The plain of Askelon is famous as the field on which the Saracens were defeated by Godfrey of Bouillon in 1099, and where Richard the First gained a signal victory over Saladin … . Askelon was a bishopric in the early ages of Christianity; but, after the expulsion of the Christians, it ceased to be a place of any importance … . It is now a place of still less note, except that the deserted ruins, and the poor village of shepherds beside the walls, remain as an evidence of the fulfilment of the prophecy, 'Askelon shall be a desolation, it shall not be inhabited, and the sea coast shall be dwellings and cottages for shepherds, and folds for flocks'.

Askelon

This was one of the five main Philistine towns. Herod the Great was born here when it was under the protection of the Roman Empire, and it was during his reign that many fine buildings were constructed. During the Third Crusade, Richard the Lionheart won back the city that had been largely destroyed by Saladin; the city walls date from this time. The Egyptian Mamelukes destroyed Askelon in 1270 and it remained a ruin until recent times.

25-26 March

25 March

Having to find our way to our tents before night we passed Ashdod by moonlight; it is a small village with no remains. Leaving our encampment by daybreak we passed a beautifully situated little village on a rising hill in the midst of the plain called Ibrieth and at last we arrived at Jaffa.

Kinnear: We reached the town about three o'clock, and set up our tents without the walls, in preference to seeking the hospitality of one of the convents. The town is surrounded by a wall, apparently of no great strength, flanked with towers at intervals … . From the inequality of the ground on which the town is built, most of the streets are paved in steps, like those of Valetta; the buildings are very much crowded together, and the interior by no means corresponds with the picturesque appearance of the town from a distance.

26 March

The approach to it is beautiful. It is surrounded by orange groves and is situated at the brow of a hill sloping towards the sea. A wall surrounds it. Today our fellow traveller Mr Kinnear took his departure for Beirout along the coast. I feel regret at parting with a countryman and such a pleasant fellow traveller. We smoked a pipe with the Consul … . I examined the town carefully but there are very few antiquities. Tomorrow we set out for the Holy City.

Kinnear: The quarantine being over at Jerusalem, my friends determined to proceed thither; but, as the journey from Egypt had occupied more time than I had anticipated, and I was very anxious to reach Beyrout without delay, I most unwillingly made up my mind to part from them here, and to take the route along the coast to Tyre and Sidon. After our long wanderings in the desert, where all are so dependant on each other for comfort, I felt sad enough at parting with my fellow travellers; some of whom I shall probably never see again; but who will remain associated, in my mind, with some of the most interesting recollections of my life. Many a happy and joyous hour we spent together, in spite of all the privations and discomforts of a desert journey.

Jaffa, Ancient Joppa

This is now the modern city of Tel Aviv. According to tradition, Noah's son founded Jaffa 40 years after the Flood and there are many stories of mythology and legend associated with the site. The rock from which Perseus rescued Andromeda was thought by the Greeks to be in the sea near the harbour, and Jonah was believed to have set out to sea from here before he was shipwrecked and swallowed by the whale.

Its turbulent history was first recorded in the 15th century BC, when it was captured by the Egyptian pharaoh, Tuthmosis III. During the Crusades it was the port used by pilgrims bound for Jerusalem, but its slow decline began after its recapture by the Muslims in 1268.

27-28 March

27 March

Left Jaffa at 10, Mr P-, our guide Ishmael, a black help and three servants to carry tents and baggage, eight horses. For these we pay 30 piastres each, this is very high but the Consul having made the bargain there is no disputing it. His attention to us has been so great and entirely without a chance of remuneration; his only gain for doing all he could for strangers being an exemption from certain rates, amongst others I believe that of the conscription.

Our way today lay through the beautiful orange gardens by which Jaffa is surrounded, and across the Plain of Sharon through a richly cultivated country. Since childhood I have not felt such a perfect enjoyment of the beauties of nature and this exhilaration of spirits can only I think be felt by those who have passed through the desert to this beautiful country. The ground seems carpeted with wild flowers and the country, independent of its great interest is the most lovely I have ever beheld.

28 March

Night found us encamped outside the walls of the City of Sion. What scenes have been enacted round the very spot which we now occupy. All is perfectly silent except the baying of a watch dog. An owl sits hooting upon the battlements, fit emblem of its desolation. The pestilence has raged within its walls for the last five months and prudence might well whisper to us to avoid it, but I cannot overcome the longing desire I have to see the great city.

Jerusalem from the Road to Bethany

Jerusalem has been the scene of innumerable historical and religious events and is a holy city to three religions: Christianity, Judaism and the Muslim faith. King David established the city as capital of the Hebrews around 1,000 BC but in the centuries that followed it has been fought over many times, and was frequently besieged and pillaged.

In 587 BC King Nebuchadnezzar invaded and led many of the defeated inhabitants into their Babylonian Captivity. The rebuilding which followed the ending of the Captivity made Jerusalem a city of palaces, theatres, temples and citadels. The Roman Emperor Titus destroyed it in 70 AD and the layout of the Old City, seen by Roberts and still in existence today, dates from 135 AD when the Emperor Hadrian established the city of Aelia Capitolina. Battling over the area continued for centuries and finally the Jews were forbidden to live there. They slowly began to return in the 13th century, and by the time of Roberts's visit there was a population of about 16,000, which included 6,000 Jews, 5,000 Muslim Arabs and 3,000 Christian Arabs.

29 March

There is an old saying that 'it is better to be born lucky than rich'. The latter has certainly not been my lot but of the former I have had my share and not the least of it since leaving England .... There have I been wandering around this unfortunate city with the most ardent desire to approach it allways deterred by the dread of being put into a quarantine after leaving — which from my experiences in Spain I have every reason to be fearful of. The moment I arrive here determined to enter at all hazard, lo and behold the quarantine is at an end and at daybreak this morning the soldiers were busied in removing the barriers and the whole population poured out of the gates, once more to enjoy the open country.

First the different troops were marched out, drums beating and colours flying. These were followed by men, women and children, not the least delighted were a group of Jews who took their station near our tents and stretching forth seemed to return thanks once more for the pure air of heaven.

The whole country is in the pure budding beauty of Spring. I cannot imagine why travellers represent it as arid or desolate or yet as being surrounded by mountains. There is really the same succesion of low hills which seem to extend all round the Plain of Sharon, all of them being cultivated to their summits, and the valley generally covered with olive grounds.

In addition to the horrors of the plague itself, the unfortunate inhabitants have been cooped up within the walls for nearly a year, the gates during this time having only been opened for two months.

For the last 30 days the pestilence has died but should it again make its appearance the same restrictions will again be enforced, but at present they are enjoying their freedom and all is holyday.

This morning I made the circuit of the walls proceeding north west by the Gate of Damascus.

Above: Damascus Gate

The most ornate and extravagant of the mediaeval gates into Jerusalem, the Damascus Gate was built in 1537 by the Turk, Suleiman the Magnificent, who also built the city walls.

Right: Pool of Bethesda

Traditionally the site of Jesus's healing of the lame man, these pools were part of the city's early water system. Excavation since Roberts's day has revealed that there were two pools separated by a dam. There was a porch on each side of the pools and a fifth on the dam, thus verifying St John's words that 'there is at Jerusalem by the sheep market a pool which is called in the Hebrew tongue Bethesda having five porches'.

29 March

The Holy Sepulchre

In the year 326 when Jerusalem was established as a Christian City, Helena, mother of the Emperor Constantine, is traditionally believed to have found the True Cross and identified the site of Christ's crucifixion and burial. Constantine erected a shrine at the spot and the first basilica was consecrated in the fourth century. Destroyed by the Persians in 614, it was rebuilt by the Byzantines and then demolished by the Caliph Hakim of Egypt in the 11th century.

The Crusaders completed a new structure that was dedicated in 1149. The building has undergone alteration and additions over the centuries and the interior is now a maze of many chapels, presided over by no fewer than six religious sects. Five years prior to Roberts's visit, there was a tragedy within the church itself when more than 100 people were trampled to death at a ceremony on Easter Eve at which the Resurrection is symbolized by the lighting of the 'Holy Fire', within the Sepulchre.

This morning I made the circuit of the walls, proceeding northwards by the Gate of Damascus, the Valley of Jehosophat to the Hill of Sion where is the tomb of David, a Mahomedan mosque which no Christian is allowed to enter. Ismael went in and described it as much neglected and a complete ruin. There were numerous pilgrims to the various objects of devotion around; they appeared to be principally Greeks, but some Armenians and a few even from Hungary. There are said to be from 4 to 5000 now in the city for the Easter festival. We visited the Latin and Armenian convents in the hopes of finding accommodation but were unsuccessful, there being in the Armenian convent alone 1300 pilgrims. Fortunately we met with Elias, the head of the only Christian family in Hebron, whose family received us there so kindly. He immediately offered us apartments at his brother-in-law's, a Greek Christian, which we willingly accepted.

We visited the different objects of attraction within the walls, the outside of the Mosque of Omer built on the site of the temple, the pool of Bethesda and the Jewish quarter and amongst others the Holy Sepulchre. It is approached through a succession of narrow streets, the last of which opens into a court in front of the principle entrance. This, with the Greek Church on Mount Calvary, I imagine are the only portions remaining of the ancient structure after its destruction by fire. The court and approach to it was quite a bazaar, filled with the merchants and pilgrims buying and selling crosses, rosaries, staffs and other things connected with the place; the crowd was very great and all was bustle and confusion. The ancient structure must have been exceedingly beautiful, of its style.

1-2 April

1 April

Having with considerable difficulty obtained horses, taking only my portmanteau, servant and tent I left about 10 o'clock for Jericho. Crossing the Valley of Jehosophat and ascending the Mount of Olives our way led through the now wretched village of Bethany … . At the bottom of the hills is the ancient site of Jericho, but I could discover no trace whatever of the town although from my situation I could command a whole view of the valley beneath. Here the governor of Jerusalem passed us attended by a gay cavalcade of military followers. He beckoned me to join him but as I was adjusting my saddle which had got out of order … I declined, & promised to pay my respects in his tent … .

Opposite was a small tower around which were scattered a few miserable houses or sheds; this I was told was Jericho! Spurring my horse that I might make a sketch while the daylight yet lingered, I crossed the brook to ride round this ruined tower being doubtful whether I had not altogether mistaken the place. Some Arab soldiers were stationed round it who immediately made signs for me not to approach too near, so much for the quarantine being taken off. The tower is Saracenic and of no great antiquity & having gained my object I returned by a different way and nearer the stream, here I found indications of ancient walls apparently of great breadth but I could not distinguish any large stones: the ruins of these foundations seem to extend a great way … . I was most politely received by the Governor and served with sherbet and coffee. I mentioned my wish to have a guide to Saint Saba and Bethlehem, he immediately acceded to it.

2 April

Our encampment was soon buried in sleep as the night came on, though occasionally I caught the sounds of the song and dance either from the pilgrims or our Arab guard. The night was one of the most beautiful I have ever seen in that country and the moon was reflected in all its brilliance in the silent waters of the Dead Sea. I lay down with my tent door open watching the lights flitting from tent to tent and wondering at the combination of creeds from all nations … .

Long before two the whole host was in motion and at 3 a gun gave signal that the Governor had left … . Lights were carried before the governor, the moon was obscured by dark clouds but its light now and then burst upon the long cavalcade seen as far as the eye could reach. All moved on in silence and the heavy tread of the dense mass was the only sound that broke the stillness of the desert. Morning at last began to dawn & the scene did not lose by the change but was even more interesting. As we approached the brink of the river a general rush took place and the women broke into the loud shrill cry of joy so often heard in Egypt. Even the camels though heavily loaded joined in the race and could scarcely be restrained by the mounted Arabs. The Governor's carpets were spread on a high bank close to the river where we could command a view of the whole. The military band and colours were placed around him and seats were assigned to us on his left. I was much struck by the great breadth of the plain of Jericho and the narrow space in which the deep and rapid river is cooped up between steep banks.

Jericho

Jericho's history stretches back as far as around 10,000 BC, when a nomadic population first settled down in this area to rear crops and domesticate animals. Jericho can also claim to be the first walled city in the world. Archaeologists have worked on the site since the 1860s, looking for traces of the walls destroyed when Joshua led the Israelites to capture Jericho around 1200 BC. These show layer upon layer of ruined mud brick walls but no definite evidence of the overthrow of the walls. Today the modern visitor can see the vast trenches dug in the 1950s by Kathleen Kenyon, the British archaeologist.

2 April

A young Greek confident in his strength was one of the first to spring into the river; he struck boldly out into the current but in the space of a second was hurried into its vortex. He strove nobly to regain the shore but the eddies caused by the rush of the immense body of water dragged him downwards; for a moment his hands were lifted from the water and after a short struggle the lifeless body was hurried on to the waters of the Dead Sea. This happened in the sight of thousands but so intent were they on their immersion that not the slightest attempt was made to save him.

Above: Bathing in the Jordan

After visiting the Holy sites within Jerusalem the Easter pilgrims joined together in a procession of many nations to bathe in the River Jordan. The garments worn by the women during the ritual immersion were preserved and used as shrouds upon their death.

Right: Descent to the Valley of the Jordan

The Jordan rift valley has frequently served as a political border. Traditionally the view of this valley from the east was the only sight of the 'Promised Land' granted to Moses. Roberts sketched it from the west but due to political unrest was unable to cross into Syria.

2-5 April

2 April

Wishing to visit the Dead Sea we sent to the Governor for a couple of soldiers as guides which he immediately granted us. Having to pass his tent where he was at his midday meal he beckoned us in and we were forced to join him. Before him was an immense pilaff garnished with sundry pieces of a whole sheep; close by it was a second dish little inferior in size to the first, of rice and milk. I followed the example of the Governor himself, thrust in my whole hand and catching as much as my five fingers could contain, conveyed it to my mouth as well as I could but not with his dexterity. If awkward at this I was still worse at tearing the flesh in pieces from a joint with my fingers; being at last presented with a spoon I confined myself to the rice and milk which I found excellent. After taking our leave we set out from Jericho for the Dead Sea, & reached it in about two hours. ... We bathed and I found the water as buoyant as it has always been represented to be by most travellers for after floating for some time on my back I had some difficulty in getting my feet again under water. The water is very bitter, making the flesh smart and most painful if it gets in the eyes.

Convent of St. Saba

3 April

Being provided with three Bedowins as guides we left Jericho for the west side of the Dead Sea ... . We enquired of our guides if it was at all practicable to reach the monastery by the route between the mountains and the sea and they reluctantly replied that it was ... .

In riding across this flat space of earth or rather mud, being a sort of delta upon a minor scale ... my horse sank to the saddle girths in deep slime ... I must say I narrowly escaped with my life for with difficulty I extricated my horse & retraced my steps as if I had been treading on eggs ... .

We descended into Wady el Haar (the Valley of Fire) through which flows the brook Kedron, then dried up, and over which is situated the convent. ... We arrived in sight of the two solitary towers overhanging the convent of St. Saba. It is situated on the brink of a deep ravine at the foot of which flows the brook, so deep that the sun's rays even at noon scarcely penetrate it. All the rocks bordering this valley are perforated with the cells of anchorites in thousands. The convent encloses the cell of one of the most renowned of these holy men. It is a cluster of buildings clinging up the face of the rock ... . The brotherhood is of the Greek persuasion and consists of about 35 monks.

5 April

It is impossible to imagine a scene more wild than the dell in which the convent is situated; the depth of the ravine must be from 4 to 500 feet and all above is wild and uncultivated, though now covered with grass and flowers; in a month or two hence when all is burnt up it must have a most desolate appearance. In looking down from the heights above on this wild place one would scarcely imagine it possessed so many comforts & conveniences within its walls. Like all the Greek convents, the rooms are fitted up as divans with the richest carpets and to us, after our arrival from the wild scenery in the neighbourhood of the Dead Sea seemed almost like enchantment ... .

I asked permission to make a sketch of their beautiful chapel which was immediately granted and though they were about to begin the service long before I had finished they would not allow me to put my book away. Leaving a donation for the poor pilgrims which is the usual mode of payment for accommodation we took our leave of the friendly monks of St. Saba and at midday we set out on our way to Bethlehem.

5-6 April

5 April

It is about 3 hours ride from St. Saba through the same kind of country but the views from the heights are even more beautiful. One or two Arab encampments are to be seen with numerous flocks grazing around. Cultivation began to appear as we approached Bethlehem, and its immediate neighbourhood abounds with fields of corn, olive and fig trees covering the sides of the hills. The Church of the Nativity crowns the height on which the town is situated and around it and attached to it are the Latin, Greek and Armenian convents. We repaired to the Latin and unfortunately found the monks in quarantine, the rooms they showed us into seemed wretched after our last abode but the two monks who were at liberty made up in kindness & attention for their indifferent accommodation. They had lost two of the brothers by plague and one cannot blame them for their precautions ... . The Church of the Nativity is in form very similar to the basilica church of Saint Paul at Rome ... . A temporary screen divides the nave from the transepts and choir, and in the latter is the Greek church which appears to be nearly as old as the rest of the Church. In the transept are the chapels of the Armenians & Latins which are very poor, immediately beneath the former is the Chapel of the Nativity, the space is exceedingly small and hung with lamps but seems poor after that of Mount Sinai. The monks say the most valuable lamps are at Jerusalem and are only suspended here upon great festivals, they being afraid if left here the Greeks or Armenians would steal them!

6 April

This day the Greek monks go through the same deception as at Jerusalem of receiving the holy fire which they pretend comes from Heaven. Whilst I was making my sketch of the interior of the chapel a man arrived from Jerusalem with the sacred fire. The whole of the Greek inhabitants turned out to receive him carrying banners & headed by their priests — all were soon in the greatest state of excitement & struggling to obtain the first light.

Above: Bethlehem looking towards the Dead Sea

Right: Shrine of the Nativity

Constantine erected a shrine over the cave where, according to tradition, Christ had been born. Caves were frequently used as stables in those days. The Byzantine Emperor, Justinian, built a basilica on the site in the sixth century, and despite the fluctuating fortunes of Bethlehem in the following centuries, the church has miraculously survived until the present day. A silver star in the shrine floor marks the traditional place of the birth.

8-10 April

8 April

This morning our fellow travellers Mr P- and Ismael Effendi took leave of us they taking the road to Cairo by the way of Hebron. In many ways I have not enjoyed so much pleasure and excitement as since leaving Egypt, the real interest of the scenes we have passed being augmented by the delightful society of my fellow travellers … .

A disturbance took place in the town from the misconduct of the military who not content with beating the men, drove the women to the convent for shelter, our two monks were called upon to quell the riot and P- and I with Ismael Effendi sallied out armed to the teeth and represented ourselves as empowered by the Pasha, we at last brought them to their reason and from what has since taken place at Jerusalem were probably the means of putting an end to much of that persecution and exaction that has been so long practised on the unfortunate inhabitants of Bethlehem … .

On our way from Bethlehem to Jerusalem we met with a great many pilgrims on their way to the birthplace of our Saviour. Midway between Bethlehem and Jerusalem is a Greek convent dedicated I think to St John from which both towns can be seen. The country is nearly all of the same character as that about Jerusalem but well cultivated.

About midday I arrived at Jerusalem and took up my abode at our worthy hosts … . In the afternoon I walked through the Valley of Jehosophat and examined the Tombs of Absalom and Zachariah. It is singular that these should be the very counterparts of those at Petra in size & shape and are also cut out of the rock.

9 April

War has broken out in the frontiers and I fear it will put a stop to my journey to Damascus. Syria must be done but Palmyra will I fear fall to the lot of someone more fortunate.

10 April

After making four drawings of the Holy Sepulchre I waited upon the new Consul, Mr Young who only arrived here today. Met Mr B- who brought a letter from V- concerning Ismael warning him not to return to Cairo as he left without permission of Abbas Pasha.

Absalom's Pillar

This monument stands outside the eastern walls of Jerusalem in the Kidron Valley, the slopes of which are littered with tombstones. These are the graves of Jews, Christians and Muslims, all awaiting the Day of Judgement. For centuries, the monument was believed to be the tomb of Absalom and followers of the three religions would throw stones and curse the monument to this disloyal son of King David. As Roberts himself realized, it should in fact be placed in the Hellenistic Age of the third or second centuries BC, when the Greeks dominated the city of Jerusalem. The nearby tomb of Zachariah also belongs to the same period. Absalom's Pillar can be seen in many of Roberts's studies of Jerusalem from this angle but he omits the white tombstones.

11-12 April

11 April

Received a letter from Captain N- with a packet of tea which was most acceptable. Dined with R- and some young Jewish missionaries.

12 April

On my return home, after sketching, I found that the Consul had done me the honour of calling with all his tail 6 Janissaries!! I began to be very tired of Jerusalem, surely there cannot be any city more wretched. How has the mighty fallen! I have wandered over the hills today in the burning sun, to find a good view of the once mighty city, but without success, the walls being almost all that is visible; within them all is misery, a third of the ground is unoccupied, about a third is built upon and another is covered with ruins which are not even picturesque. All the mosques including the celebrated Omer are fast falling to ruins.

Jerusalem from the Mount of Olives

Jerusalem achieved prominence as a Christian city in the fourth and fifth centuries AD under the Byzantine Empire, but it was to suffer many changes of rulers in its troubled history. In 1099 the soldiers of the First Crusade took Jerusalem from the Seljuk Turks, who were preventing Christian pilgrims from visiting the Holy City, and founded the Kingdom of Jerusalem. Less than a century later, in 1187, Saladin captured the city, and resisted the attempts by Richard the Lionheart and the Third Crusaders to regain control. The Crusaders did achieve a short period of occupation during the 13th century but the rulers for by far the longest period were the Ottoman Turks, who ruled from 1517 until 1917. However, at the time of Roberts's visit, Syria was governed by local Turkish pashas, but the suzerainty of the whole area was in the hands of Mehemet Ali, Pasha of Egypt, who had invaded in 1831. He remained in control until 1840 when England, as an ally of the Turks, defeated him and compelled him to hand Syria back to the Ottoman Empire. It was these struggles between Egypt and the Turks which led to Roberts abandoning his plans to visit Damascus and Palmyra.

12 April

It has been a melancholy enjoyment for me to wander round these walls and ponder over the past … . There are two entrances to the enclosure on which stands the Mosque of Omer on the west side, and this part of the wall which is held most sacred is about one hundred feet to the south of the southern of the two entrances, and is partly hidden by houses. Here the stones are of equal magnitude with those of the east & south sides, but from being partly concealed by the houses are probably in better preservation. The Jews still resort here at stated periods from whence they announce to their brethren, as the sons of Levi did of old from the temple walls, that the feast of the passover was about to commence. I was taken to this part by one of the young Jewish converts who have just taken up their abode here. He informed me that this part of the temple, facing the hill of Sion, is the part still held in the greatest veneration and even when he himself beheld it as a Polish Jew & a Christian his eyes were so filled with tears that he could distinguish nothing around him. The unfortunate Jews cannot even pray here in peace but are pelted with stones whilst in the very act and every insult is heaped upon the unfortunate remnant that still lingers within the city of David … .

The Mosque of Omer was described to me by Ismael Effendi after his visit, not having seen Burckhardt's description of it I do not know how far it may agree with it. The effect of the ceiling of the great Dome is very fine being covered as is the outside with painted tiles. The tesselated pavement belonged to the church at Bethlehem built by the Empress Helena but was removed here by the Caliph Omer. In the centre of the Dome stands a great rock in the rough state, to which they say the Prophet fastened his camel that carried him from here to Mount Sinai (where I was shown the mark of his hoof on the rock) and from thence to Mecca in an incredible short time; there is a hole in the rock which is shown, to which it was attached. Previous to beginning the journey he rested in a cave immediately underneath which is also shown and once in rising in the attitude of prayer, the rock on top which was too low for his height gave way so that he could stand erect, leaving the indentation of his skull in the solid rock! On his ascent a part of the rock, seized with a desire I suppose to perform the same journey went up after him to ask forgiveness I cannot say for what, but having obtained it, it returned like a sensible rock and took up its old place as before.

Mosque of Omer

The gilded Dome of the Rock, which is still incorrectly referred to as the Mosque of Omer, is one of the most important and best preserved examples of Muslim architecture. In 638 AD the followers of Mohammed conquered Jerusalem; the city was still in ruins following its brutal sack by the Persians in 614. In 691 the Muslim Caliph Omer decided to build a shrine to rival Mecca and Medina and the construction of the Dome of the Rock began. Using the Church of the Holy Sepulchre as inspiration, it consists of an octagonal base surmounted by a gilded dome; the dome seen by Roberts dated from 1022 when the original one, supposedly made of solid gold, collapsed. Its site was chosen because it was believed to be the place from which Mohammed began his journey to Heaven. To the Jews it was the site of Abraham's sacrifice of Isaac. Suleiman the Magnificent covered the eight-sided base with richly-coloured tiles and the interior is exquisitely decorated with Byzantine mosaics. The mosque was restored between 1958 and 1964 and the dome recovered in gilt aluminium.

13 April

Waited upon the new Consul Mr Young who is the first Consul of any nation who has taken up his residence within the walls of Jerusalem … . The Sirocco or south wind is raging here today. The whole atmosphere is impregnated with particles of sand from the desert and is not only disagreeable in itself but seems to have an effect upon the spirits making everyone restless.

I have never had more uphill work than in sketching the various objects of interest about Jerusalem. The city within the walls may be called a desert, two thirds of it being a mess of ruins and cornfields; the remaining third, with its bazaars and ruined mosques being of such a paltry and contemptible character that no artist could render them interesting. Even the Holy Sepulchre itself comes under this head, the fire of 1810 having destroyed everything like architecture about it and it is now replaced by the most monstrous jumble of walls, arches and domes that could be put together by a people just emerging from barbarism, even the far famed Mosque of Omer is externally at least a tawdry piece of finery fast hastening to ruin. It is covered with painted tile all but the dome and of this the lead is torn off in many places. On comparing the stones still remaining of the great temple with the super abundant rubbish heaped over them I have often laid down my pencil in despair. The

spots pointed out by the zeal of the Christians are nearly all very doubtful. Some even doubt whether the Holy Sepulchre with all its enclosures covers the site of Calvary.

Mount Mariah alone seems certain where Abraham offered up his son Isaac, here Solomon built a temple to the God of Israel; here took place the dire conflicts between the sons of Jacob and their enemies although, probably according to the prophecy, scarce one stone is left upon another yet the wall of the enclosure still remains a monument of its strength and vastness.

Entrance to the Citadel

The Citadel is the area in the south-west of Jerusalem where Herod the Great built his palace. In those days, a deep valley separated this hill from the temple mount where Herod constructed the temple visited by Jesus and destroyed by the Emperor Titus in 70 AD. To connect the two, Herod erected two viaducts but very little of these remain.

The Crusaders fortified the Citadel and when Suleiman the Magnificent built the city walls in the 16th century, he included a gate near the site — the Jaffa Gate.

15-17 April

15 April

Mr N- having joined me we started for Nablous with three mules each. We left Jerusalem at 9am and in the evening pitched our tents in a beautiful Wady here. Passing about midday the town of Beer with a ruined Christian church. The day was hot and sultry and at night our tent was surrounded by jackals. The country around is cultivated to the very summits of the hills and the valleys are beautiful abounding with olive and vine plantations.

16 April

We started at day break though the morning was wet and drizzling, and passing through a finely cultivated country we arrived at Nablous, ancient Shechem about 3 o'clock. The approach to it is through a long avenue of ancient olive trees and the situation of the town is beautiful.

Placed between the two celebrated mountains it is sheltered from the north and south winds. Vegetation seemed much more advanced here than in any part of the road we had hitherto passed.

The town is large & populous and the inhabitants appear to be better off than most I have seen in Palestine.

17 April

Nablous is by far the most beautiful town I have seen in Syria, in point of situation, it lies in the midst of gardens and is intersected in every direction by streams of the most limpid water, rendering it rich & fertile when contrasted with the naked mountains round it. ... The gardens abound with orange, citron, fig and pomegranates, & beyond these are meadows covered with the richest pasture whilst the sides of the mountains are cultivated with corn & olive grounds extending to the valley in which is situated Sebaste. ... visited the synagogue, the only remnant left of the ancient Samaritans. It stands in an obscure part of the town. After knocking for some time we were admitted & were then shown with great care two manuscripts of the Pentateuch, one 500 years old, the other 3,000 BC, this is considered unique. They were both in the form of scrolls enclosed in a rich chased tabernacle either of brass or gold of the most antique workmanship ... .

We engaged a couple of Arabs to conduct us to the well of Jacob where the interview took place between our Saviour and the woman of Samaria. It is now a heap of ruins and the shafts of several granite columns half buried but in an upright position, sticking through the rubbish are all the remains of the edifice erected over it by the Empress Helena.

Entrance to Nablous

Shekhem, which is just south east of Nablous on a crossroads of main routes, was important even in the time of the Canaanites, when Abraham camped here and built the first altar. In the 13th century BC, Joshua assembled the tribes of Israel at Shekhem and made his last address. After the death of Solomon, Jeroboam broke away from the union with Judah and created a new capital at Shekhem for the ten Northern tribes of Israel. Despite persecution since the eighth century BC, there has always been a Samaritan community in Nablous and Shekhem was at one time their capital.

The scroll seen by Roberts was unlikely to be 3,000 years old, as the Pentateuch is thought not to have been committed to writing until the time of the Babylonian exile in the sixth century BC. Archaeological excavations of the 20th century have uncovered extensive ruins from biblical times, all of which would have been hidden beneath Roberts's feet.

19-20 April

19 April

A winding path leads you up into the mountain and after a ride of about an hour and a half you descend upon the beautiful hamlet of Nazareth nestled as it were in the bosom of the hills by which it is surrounded. The Latin convent forms the most conspicuous part of the village; here, we were kindly received by the superior and took up our residence. I found H- and L- had left at midday for Mount Carmel having visited Taberia but obliged to abandon the way to Damascus by the bridge of Joseph ... . Ibrim Pasha has left with his army for the frontiers, the restless inhabitants having broken out in fresh insurrection are seizing all they can lay hands on.

20 April

Made two coloured drawings of the interior of the chapel, one of the grotto or Chapel of the Annunciation and also two views of the town. Besides the convent there are several other objects of interest pointed out to the pilgrim: the workshop of Joseph; the stone on which Christ sat with his disciples, the visiting of which earns the pious Catholic 40 years indulgence, the rock over which the Nazarenes threw our Saviour, and the only fountain in Nazareth, where the Virgin is said to have gone for water. This fountain, with the groups of young women round it carrying their water jars was more suited for a picture than anything I have seen in the Holy Land. I returned to our convent as the sun was setting, and after a hearty meal with the superior, a Spaniard, I retired to prepare for the morrow's journey to Tabaria.

A General View of Nazareth

Mentioned in the New Testament as a 'town on the mountain', Nazareth lies on the southern edge of the Galilean mountains, on the Plain of Yesreel. The town was established as a Christian centre of pilgrimage by Constantine in the fourth century, and Jesus lived there until he was baptized. The town was captured by the Muslims in 636 but they agreed to respect churches and synagogues and the Christian settlement, although small, remained.

The Crusaders took Nazareth in 1099 and began major reconstruction work. Although Saladin occupied the town in 1187, he did not destroy the Christian buildings. In the years that followed, the town fluctuated between Muslim and Christian rule until the latter half of the 13th century, when the Crusaders finally lost control and much of Nazareth was destroyed.

The Franciscans were allowed to return in the 16th century when they attempted to identify the sites associated with the childhood of Christ. In 1620, they established a monastery there and it was their successors who were such hospitable hosts to Roberts, despite the fact that their monastery had been extensively damaged by an earthquake.

21 April

Left Nazareth at 11 and after a pleasant ride of about an hour and a half we arrived at Cana of Galilee. Like most of the villages of Palestine it is situated on the slope of a hill, but is a miserable place consisting only of about 40 or 50 houses and the most of them in ruins. At the bottom of the hill is a small Greek church; as we were passing it, an old man came out and showed us a written document of the names of the various travellers who had recently visited Cana. We went into the church and he showed us, built into the wall <u>the identical</u> jar that had held the water turned into wine at the marriage feast! The church itself is said to cover the spot formerly occupied by the house in which this miracle took place.

Above: Chapel of the Annunciation

The church drawn by Roberts dated from about 1730 when the Franciscans were allowed to build a new church — the fourth on the same site. It was demolished in the 1950s and the church that now stands there was consecrated in 1969.

Right: The Fountain of the Virgin, Nazareth

The present fountain of this name was built in 1882 and remodelled in 1967. It does not stand on precisely the same site as the one Roberts drew, which was reputed to have been used by the Virgin Mary.

21-22 April

21 April

Passing through a beautiful country in about five hours we came in sight of the Sea of Galilee embossomed in the surrounding hills. Far to the left is Mount Hermon covered with snow and nearer to us is Saffet; here it is expected by the Jews the Messiah is to reign 40 years before entering Jerusalem ... . The Sea of Galilee was the scene of most of our Saviour's miracles, his walking on the water, the draught of fishes and his teaching the multitude. Here the disciples plied their humble calling of fishermen. Not a boat is now to be seen upon its surface.

To the South the Jordan flows from the lake to the Dead Sea and immediately at our feet and close to the lake lay the town of Taberia. During the time our tents were pitched we strolled into the town. It is encircled with a wall flanked with towers but we were astonished to find that all within was a mass of ruins with a few temporary huts erected in the middle. The town with 400 of its inhabitants was destroyed by an earthquake about two and a half years ago. Its present inhabitants are nearly all Jews who come here to die ... . They live in expectation of the reappearance of the Messiah and are supported by contributions made by their brethren in different parts of the world.

22 April

Made several sketches of the town or rather its remains for every part of it has been more or less injured by earthquakes. The part nearest the lake seemed to have suffered most; the city wall, which is built of hewn square stones, is in most parts thrown down and those remaining are rent from top to bottom ... . Though I saw the skeleton of an ancient boat I looked in vain for an ancient fisherman! The hills around only want wood to complete the beauty of the scene ... . Towards midday we left for Mount Carmel, and at night very tired, rested by the only fountain in Cana.

Left: Fountain of Cana

Above: Tiberias looking towards the Lebanon

Ancient Tiberias was founded about 19 AD by Herod Antipas and named in honour of the Roman Emperor. Because it had been built on the site of a Jewish cemetery, it was considered unclean and even Jesus, who taught widely in this area, did not visit it. It was subsequently declared ritually clean and from the third century AD, it became the religious centre of the Jews; the tombs of many famous rabbis can still be seen. The Crusaders rebuilt Tiberias on a new site to the north but the town suffered much in the earthquake of 1837 and many of its inhabitants were killed. The walls Roberts mentioned were later demolished and only the occasional picturesque tower left standing.

23-25 April

23 April

We left at half past 7 for Acre, passing through part of the most fertile country I have ever seen .... About three we came in sight of St Jean d'Acre with the blue Mediterranean. The situation is beautiful forming a promontory to the north of the bay, Mount Carmel forming the other to the south. A large ship of war lay in the offing, and the fortifications of Acre rising above the plain on which it stands, with the blue sea beyond formed a picture which would have satisfied Turner himself.

Pitching our tents on a piece of ground bordering the sea and in front of the ramparts we strolled into the town. Its fortifications are strong and the walls of a great height ... they appear to have suffered greatly during the late seige, part of them having just been repaired. The houses in the town have if possible suffered more than the outworks, one half being in ruins and most of the principal mosques burnt or fallen down during the bombardment.

24 April

After making two sketches of the town R- and I rode round the bay to Carmel which is distant from here about three leagues in a

circuitous line; the bay being two leagues in breadth ... I counted no less than 13 vessels wrecked some of them merely skeletons. We crossed the brook Kishara immortalized in the Song of Deborah and in three hours approached the town of Caipha. Judging from the outside this is a pretty town for Syria and in good condition ... . On our arrival at the gate they refused us admittance when they heard we had come from Acre, the plague having broken out again at Jaffa. We passed the town and ascended Mount Carmel where after a little delay we were received by the monks there with great kindness.

25 April

A heavy rain in the morning obliged us to wait until the middle of the day before we could leave here, and the greater part of it was taken up in passing over the remainder of the plain of Acre and we found in our approach to Cape Blanco that we could not pass it before nightfall, we therefore pitched our tents near an ancient Roman fountain of which only a few stones were left. The night was cold and the ground damp and uncomfortable quite a place for catching ague and a hundred other things.

St Jean d'Acre from the Sea

Acre was originally founded by the Phoenicians but throughout its long and violent history, it has been captured by many different warring factions and it has played a major role in the struggle for power in the Middle East. The Crusaders made it the headquarters of the Knights of St John, hence its name. Its destruction by the Muslims in 1291 signalled the end of the Crusader Wars.

Re-building began in the 18th century and a new city rose from the ruins, strong enough to withstand Napoleon's siege in 1799. However, the Egyptian Pasha, Ibrahim, besieged the town again not long before Roberts visited Acre and obviously caused much damage. A year after his visit, the combined fleets of Turkey, England and Austria bombarded Acre.

26-28 April

26 April

A few hours ride along the sands brought us in front of ancient Tyre or rather the ancient site of it. The plain is not of very great extent and is boarded on the east by low hills. Some remains of the ancient city still exist, they are probably buried under the sand which is drifted along the coast to a considerable height especially the isthmus formed from its ruins by Alexander. ... The present town is a mere village with a mosque rising in the centre and the prophecy that it should become a rock for fishermen to dry their nets on is literally fulfilled ... .

27 April

Leaving Tyre about 11 ... the chain of Lebanon, now covered with snow, rises magnificently in the background. The view of Sidon, which we saw from a little farmhouse with gardens of olive and mulberry trees, is one of the finest I have ever seen in this country. ... we were stopped by a guard who demanded of us our bill of health — having been told at Jerusalem we should have no occasion for one, of course we were unprovided with it. On account of the return of the pilgrims from Jerusalem a quarantine had been established and we could proceed no

farther. Knowing that the only way to get over a difficulty in this country was to put a bold face on it, I told him that I carried a firman from the Pasha Mehemet Ali and that if they stopped me they must be answerable for the consequences ... they immediately lowered their line and I was desired to remount and proceed with a soldier as my guard.

28 April

Our guard having remained all night with us we were prevented entering the town and when we walked he kept a little before us

beating everyone out of the way and calling out we were in quarantine till the people actually thought we were plague subjects. This was a confounded annoyance but I was determined to sketch.

Above: Tyre from the Isthmus

Right: Citadel of Sidon

Tyre and Sidon were the two major cities of the Phoenicians, seamen and traders who inhabited this coastal region from c. 1200 BC and who built up a vast overseas trading empire. Tyre was originally an island with excellent harbours, until Alexander the Great joined it to the mainland with a causeway during his siege of 332 BC.

1-4 May

1 May

We now descended into a plain of vast extent far as the eye could reach, lying between the chains of Lebanon and Antilebanon: a river winds through it and every portion of it from mountain to mountain cultivated or in pasture … . Having to stop to make some purchases our servants brought the news that an insurrection had broken out at Baalbek which was very mortifying after such a laborious journey across the mountains to reach it. Buckling on our swords and looking as martial as possible we sought out the house of the Sheik who was from home but we saw the Janissary. We produced our firman which was gravely perused, coffee was served and we learnt that war had not actually broken out but that it was hourly expected.

4 May

The severe weather I had experienced in crossing Mount Lebanon by a circuitous route and sleeping on the damp ground in my tent — together with the fatigue I had undergone since leaving Cairo, going on for three months, had quite exhausted me and here at Baalbek I had a severe illness from which however thanks to God I recovered.

It would be difficult to convey even in drawing any idea of the magnificent ruin its beauty of form, the exquisite richness of its decorations or the vast magnitude of its dimensions. The measurements have often been given, I shall therefore merely offer a few general remarks on the structure itself. The whole is contained within an irregular oblong enclosure, showing that it has at one period if not always been used as a place of defence; a comparatively small portion of it is occupied by the celebrated temple, and although in a ruinous state it is still by far the most perfect as well as the most beautiful in its proportions I have ever seen … .

Behind the portico a wall of more recent date has been built so as to hide the grand doorway but creeping through a small aperture in this you stand before the splendid entrance. Its dimensions are immense and its decorations are worthy of such a structure; the lintel has been formed of three enormous stones on the principle of the arch but the centre one has slipped downwards and remains suspended between the two. The ornamental details of this door are so exquisite that it would take weeks to copy them. …

This morning I was informed by my servant that my mules were seized for the use of the government to carry corn for the troops. Having again recourse to my firman I lost no time in waiting on the Governor who I found seated on a divan surrounded by one of the most picturesque groups I have ever seen … . I produced my firman and opened the business. To my surprise no one could read it, it being in Turkish, the only intelligible part of it being the signature of Abbas Pasha, Governor of Cairo; this however was quite sufficient and he apologised for our mules being carried off, & offered to send soldiers in every direction to search for them … . Being dressed in my English clothes I was a matter of great curiosity to them & from their many enquiries I should think that a Frank is a rare sight.

Baalbek, General View

The site of Baalbek must have been sacred before Roman times but very little is known of its history. Its present Arabic name indicates pre-Roman occupation; Baal is the name of the old Seimitic deity frequently referred to in the Old Testament. The Greek name Heliopolis was probably given to it after its conquest by Alexander the Great, in the fourth century BC.

Despite its history of destruction, massacre and earthquakes, Baalbek was never totally defeated and by the middle of the 19th century, there was a steady flow of visitors to record the magnificent ruins. Six gigantic columns remain of the Temple of Jupiter but the Temple of Bacchus is in a remarkable state of preservation. Sadly, the ruins have been inaccessible to tourists since the outbreak of the Lebanese Civil War.

4-8 May

4 May

About half an hour's walk up the valley leading to the mountains through which flows the beautiful stream to which the plain owes its fertility, is the fountain from whence it springs. It rises in a great body from under the ruins of two semi-circular basins, the most pure, the most limpid & the sweetest water I have ever tasted. In the centre are the ruins of an artificial fountain probably containing at one time the statue of the goddess of the stream & near it has been a mosque which is now thrown down, probably from the fragments of columns, friezes etc. occupying the site of a temple dedicated to the same deity. It is the very spot that imagination would select for the Naiads. Here is the bubbling fountain around which the grass still seems smoother and greener than anywhere else; the mountains of Lebanon tower above, covered with eternal snow rivalling in whiteness the clouds in which they are enveloped, whilst the sides of this lovely valley are still covered with fruit trees in all the gaiety of their summer clothing.

Alas! what a change in all but nature herself — the fountain, the temple, the mosque are a mass of ruins overgrown with lichen and wild flowers through the midst of which the crystal stream still winds its way;

Right: Baalbek from the Fountain

The temple of Bacchus is larger than the Parthenon in Athens but it would have been swamped by its gigantic neighbour, dedicated to Jupiter.

Left: Doorway, Baalbek

The dramatic keystone in Roberts's illustration of the porch of the Temple of Bacchus has now been restored to its original position.

but where are the gay citizens that once frequented its banks, where the maids who resorted here to make their offerings to its protecting deity, where the wealth and plenty that once belonged to this proud city?

8 May

Little indeed has been hitherto known of this magnificent ruin … . Finishing all I had to do … we took a last look of glorious Baalbek.

11-13 May

11 May

Occupied all day arranging for my voyage to Alexandria. With the exception of my water skins & some pewter dishes, I presented my tent with all its appurtenances to my servant by way of a bucksheys.

13 May

With regrets I this morning took leave of Palestine & embarked on board the 'Magaria' for Alexandria.

Roberts's biography and letters record the following events:

During my stay here I was presented by Colonel Campbell to Mehemet Ali ...

I was early astir, breakfasted at ½ past 7, sadly puzzled how to rig myself out, being sadly in want of everything requisite for such an interview .... Mehemet Ali seated himself in one corner of the high divan which surrounded it, and beckoned us to be also seated on his left. Coffee was brought in, the service covered with a rich embroidered cloth of gold, an officer in attendance handing a cup to each guest .... Pipes were not introduced, this being an honour reserved, I am told,

only for nobility, a Lord at least .... During the whole of this interview, which lasted about twenty minutes, I had an excellent opportunity of drawing him, and duly regretted that I had not a pencil and paper that I could have made a memorandum of such a face, those hitherto taken conveying no idea of his animated countenance.

Leaving Alexandria, we reached Malta in six days, and were kept in quarantine for three weeks ... landed safely, thank God, in London, on 21st July, having been eleven months absent.

Interview with the Pasha

The interview with Mehemet Ali, under whose protection Roberts had been travelling, took place on 12 May — Roberts is third from the left in the European group.

Born in Albania, Mehemet Ali was Pasha or Viceroy of Egypt from 1805 to 1848, and also Pasha of Syria from 1833 to 1840. Although he nominally acknowledged the Turkish Sultan as ruler, the Pasha had considerable power, which was eventually restrained by an alliance of Turkey, England and Austria in 1840. The peace treaty terms stipulated that he revert to his original subservient role of ruler of Egypt alone.

He was responsible for many of the reforms which slowly brought about the modernisation of Egypt. He died in 1849, at the age of 80.

List of Lithographs

Bibliography

Ballantine, J. *The Life of David Roberts R.A.,* Edinburgh, 1866.

Baines & Malek, *Atlas of Ancient Egypt,* Oxford, 1980.

Browning, I. *Petra,* London, 1973.

Clayton, P.A. *The Rediscovery of Ancient Egypt,* London, 1982.

Fagan, B.M. *The Rape of the Nile,* London, 1975.

Galey, J. *Sinai and the Monastery of Saint Catherine,* New York, 1980.

Gilbert, M. *Jerusalem, Rebirth of a City,* London, 1985.

Guiterman, H. *David Roberts R.A.,* privately published, London, 1978.

Guiterman & Llewellyn, *David Roberts,* Barbican Exhibition, London, 1986.

James, T.G.H. *An Introduction to Ancient Egypt,* London, 1979.

Kinnear, J. *Cairo, Petra and Damascus in 1839,* London, 1841.
The Holy Land, Syria, Idumea, Arabia, Egypt and Nubia, from drawings by David Roberts R.A., London, 1842–9.

Macquitty, W. *Island of Isis,* London, 1976.

Magnusson, M. *The Archaeology of the Bible Lands,* London, 1977.

Ragette, F. *Baalbek,* London, 1980.

Richmond, J.C.B. *Egypt 1798–1952,* London, 1977.

Sim, K. *David Roberts R.A., 1796–1864. A Biography,* London, 1984.

Index